NOTHINGNESS

WHEN? WHAT? WHY?

ROMERO D' SOUZA

Made with ♥ on the Notion Press Platform
www.notionpress.com

gOd

hUmanIty

natURe

Contents

Foreword

In a world that often values material possessions and the accumulation of knowledge and information, the concept of nothingness may seem elusive, confusing, or even frightening. Yet, throughout history, philosophers, theologians, scientists, and artists have grappled with the idea of nothingness, recognizing its potential to reveal deep truths about existence, meaning, and the human experience.

In this book, the author delves into the complex and multifaceted nature of nothingness, exploring its different dimensions, from the philosophical and metaphysical to the scientific and artistic. Drawing on a wide range of sources, from ancient texts to contemporary theories, the author invites us to reconsider our assumptions about what nothingness means and how it shapes our understanding of the world and ourselves.

Through a series of thought-provoking ideas, the author gives us a peep into the When? What? Why? of nothingness, and to embrace the possibility of emptiness as a source of creativity, renewal, and freedom. Whether we are grappling with existential questions, seeking to deepen our spiritual practice, or simply curious about the nature of reality, this book offers a rich and rewarding exploration of one of the most profound and enduring concepts in human thought.

I invite you to join me in reading this book on nothingness, and to engage with its ideas, insights, and challenges. May it inspire us to see the world with fresh eyes, and to embrace the transformative potential of emptiness in our lives and in the world around us.

Z-A

Preface

The concept of nothingness has been a source of fascination and contemplation for thinkers and artists throughout history. From ancient philosophy to contemporary science, from Eastern spirituality to Western existentialism, the idea of emptiness, absence, and negation has challenged our assumptions about reality and pushed us to question our place in the world.

This book on nothingness seeks to explore the many dimensions of this elusive and enigmatic concept. The author aims to examine the role of nothingness in human thought and experience, and to uncover its potential as a source of creativity, transformation, and insight.

The approach is interdisciplinary, drawing on insights and perspectives from a wide range of fields, including philosophy, psychology, art, literature, and science. The aim is to present a diverse range of voices and perspectives, reflecting the complexity and richness of the concept of nothingness.

While the exploration of nothingness may at times be challenging or even unsettling, one may believe that it offers a valuable opportunity to confront one's deepest fears and anxieties, and to discover new ways of seeing and being in the world. Whether one is seeking to deepen one's understanding of oneself, to grapple with the big questions of existence, or simply to appreciate the beauty and mystery of life, I hope that this book will offer a thought-provoking and inspiring journey into the heart of nothingness.

I would like to thank all the people that walked into my life to teach me and give me this gift of nothingness, whose insights and reflections through the experiences and exploration of readings have enriched, enhanced, and expanded the understanding of nothingness. I also extend my earnest gratitude to the readers, whose engagement with these ideas will continue to shape and inform the ongoing conversation around nothingness and its place in their lives and in the world.

Acknowledgements

The publication of this book on NOTHINGNESS would not have been possible without the contributions, support, and encouragement of you. I would like to take this opportunity to express gratitude and appreciation to all those who have made this project a reality.

First and foremost, I would also like to thank my family, friends, and companions for their support and encouragement throughout thus far of the journey of my life. Their belief in my vision and their willingness to offer feedback and support has been instrumental in bringing this project to fruition.

I would like to thank persons all along the journey who have encouraged and criticized me to be the person that I am today. This book seeks their insights, perspectives, and creativity that have enriched and expanded my understanding of nothingness. Their willingness to share their ideas and experiences has been invaluable, and I am more than honored to have had the opportunity to work with them.

I would like to extend my gratitude to Notion Press publisher and to Amazon platform, who will bring this book to readers around the world.

Finally, I would like to thank the readers of this book, whose engagement and curiosity will continue to shape the ongoing conversation around nothingness and its place in our lives and in the world. We hope that this book will inspire new insights, new questions, and new paths of exploration, and we look forward to continuing the conversation with all those who share our passion for this fascinating and profound concept.

Prologue

In a world that often seems obsessed with productivity, achievement, and material success, the concept of nothingness can be both frightening and liberating. On the one hand, nothingness can evoke feelings of emptiness, meaninglessness, and despair. On the other hand, it can offer a doorway to freedom, creativity, and transcendence. In this book on nothingness, I invite you to explore the many dimensions of this elusive and enigmatic concept.

In his poem "The Dark Night of the Soul," St. John of the Cross (along with St. Teresa of Avila) describes the experience of nothingness as a kind of death, a letting go of all that is familiar and comfortable:

"I abandoned and forgot myself,
laying my face on my Beloved;
all things ceased;
I went out from myself,
leaving my cares forgotten among the lilies."

He saw the dark night of the soul as a process of purging oneself of all attachments and distractions, including even one's own sense of self and identity. This process involved a radical detachment from all things, including one's own desires and aspirations, in order to achieve a state of complete nothingness. The core of St. John of the Cross' teaching is "nada, nada, nada!" Basically, it means that "nothing, nothing, nothing"

My journey into nothingness begins with this examination, along with St John of the Cross and Teresa of Avila, of its philosophical roots. I explore the ideas of ancient philosophers who grappled with the nature of nothingness, from the Greek concept of kenosis to the Buddhist doctrine of emptiness.

In this book I seek to answer these 3 W's questions: **When? What? Why?**

When? skimming through the western and eastern philosophers who have lived from ancient times to the present postmodern era.

What? seeking to see through the different thoughts connected to or linked with nothingness.

Why? situating each individual in the context of a specific issue or conundrum, whether it be psychological, phenomenological, or spiritual.

Throughout this book, I aim to present a diverse range of perspectives on nothingness, drawing on insights and ideas from a wide range of fields. I also invite you to reflect on your own relationship to nothingness, and to consider how this concept might shape your own understanding of yourself and the world around you.

I hope that this book will inspire you to embrace the mysteries of nothingness, and to discover new paths of creativity, growth, and fulfilment.

Romero D'Souza

ONE

NOTHINGNESS: WESTERN AND EASTERN PHILOSOPHERS

Nothingness

What is nothingness? It is a concept that has intrigued and fascinated thinkers and artists throughout history. It is a term that seems to defy easy definition, and yet it has been explored and interpreted in countless ways.

At its most basic level, nothingness refers to the absence or nonexistence of something. It is the lack of substance or form, the absence of meaning or purpose. But nothingness is also a concept that goes beyond mere emptiness or negation. It is a fundamental aspect of our experience of the world, and a source of profound mystery and wonder.

"Nothingness" refers to the absence or lack of anything, including matter, energy, substance, or meaning. It is often associated with emptiness, void, or non-existence.

In philosophy, "nothingness" has been a subject of discussion for centuries, particularly in existentialist and nihilist thought. Some philosophers argue that the concept of nothingness is fundamental to understanding the human experience, as it emphasizes the transience and impermanence of all things.

In physics, the concept of nothingness is also important, as it relates to the nature of the universe and the fundamental particles that make up matter. The study of nothingness in physics has led to the development of theories about the nature of dark matter, dark energy, and the Big Bang.

In everyday language, the term "nothingness" is often used in a more casual sense to refer to a lack of importance or significance, as in the phrase "it was all for nothing."

Nothingness and Philosophy

In philosophy, the concept of "nothingness" has been explored by various thinkers throughout history. One of the most prominent discussions of nothingness occurred in the works of the German philosopher Martin Heidegger, who believed that nothingness was not simply the absence of something, but rather an essential aspect of being.

Heidegger argued that humans have a tendency to overlook the concept of nothingness, instead focusing on beings and the world around them. However, he believed that embracing the concept of nothingness could lead to a more authentic understanding of being and existence.

Similarly, in existentialist philosophy, the concept of nothingness is often used to explore the meaning and purpose of human existence. Jean-Paul Sartre famously argued that human beings are "condemned to freedom," meaning that they must confront the void of nothingness and create their own meaning and purpose in life.

The concept of nothingness has also been discussed in relation to the nature of reality and the universe. Some philosophers have argued that the universe could have emerged from a state of absolute nothingness, while others have suggested that nothingness is simply a mental construct or a limitation of human perception.

Overall, the concept of nothingness has been an important subject of philosophical inquiry, with various thinkers offering different perspectives on its nature and significance.

WESTERN

Nothingness and Ancient Western Philosophers

The concept of "nothingness" has been a subject of philosophical inquiry since ancient times in Western philosophy. Here are a few examples of ancient Western philosophers who explored the concept of nothingness:

1. Parmenides: Parmenides was an ancient Greek philosopher who believed that being (existence) was the only reality, and that nothingness was simply a mental construct. He argued that nothingness could not exist, because there was no way to conceive of it or describe it.

2. Plato: Plato, another ancient Greek philosopher, explored the idea of nothingness in his dialogues. In the Timaeus, for example, he describes the creation of the universe as the result of the demiurge (a divine craftsman) imposing order on a pre-existing chaos or nothingness.
3. Aristotle: Aristotle, also an ancient Greek philosopher, rejected the idea of absolute nothingness, arguing that everything that exists is a substance or a combination of substances. He believed that nothingness was simply the absence of something, and that it had no real existence in itself.
4. Epicurus: Epicurus, an ancient Greek philosopher who founded the school of Epicureanism, believed that nothingness was the natural state of things, and that everything that exists is made up of atoms and void (empty space). He argued that death should not be feared, because it simply involves the dissolution of the soul and the return to a state of nothingness.

These are just a few examples of ancient Western philosophers who explored the concept of nothingness in their works. The concept has continued to be an important subject of philosophical inquiry throughout the history of Western thought.

Nothingness and Medieval Western Philosophers

The concept of "nothingness" continued to be explored by medieval Western philosophers, particularly in the context of theological debates about the nature of God and creation. Here are a few examples of medieval Western philosophers who engaged with the concept of nothingness:

Augustine of Hippo: Augustine, a Christian philosopher and theologian, believed that nothingness was not a positive reality, but rather the absence of something that should be present. He argued that evil, for example, was not a substance or a thing, but rather the absence of good.

Thomas Aquinas: Aquinas, a Christian philosopher and theologian, also believed that nothingness was the absence of something that should be present. He argued that God was the source of all being, and that nothingness was simply the absence of God's presence.

John Duns Scotus: Scotus, a medieval Franciscan philosopher, argued that nothingness was a real possibility, and that it was necessary to account for the possibility of nothingness in order to understand the nature of creation. He believed that God's act of creation was not necessary, but rather a free choice, and that the possibility of nothingness was inherent in this freedom.

William of Ockham: Ockham, a medieval Franciscan philosopher, believed that nothingness was a real possibility, and that it was necessary to posit the existence of a God who could create ex nihilo (out of nothing). He argued that the universe was contingent and could have been different, and that the existence of nothingness was a necessary consequence of this contingency.

These are just a few examples of medieval Western philosophers who explored the concept of nothingness in the context of theological debates about the nature of God and creation. The concept of nothingness continued to be an important subject of philosophical inquiry throughout the medieval period and beyond.

Nothingness and Contemporary Western Philosophers

In contemporary Western philosophy, the concept of nothingness has been explored extensively. Here are some key ideas from influential philosophers:

1. Martin Heidegger - Heidegger believed that the experience of nothingness is fundamental to human existence. He argued that we often try to distract ourselves from the awareness of our own mortality, but that we can never truly escape the fact that we will one day cease to exist. He called this awareness "being-toward-death" and argued that it is necessary for us to confront it in order to live an authentic life.
2. Jean-Paul Sartre - Sartre was an existentialist philosopher who believed that existence precedes essence. This means that we are not born with a predetermined nature or purpose, but that we must create ourselves through our choices and actions. Sartre also argued that the experience of nothingness is a necessary part of human existence. He believed that when we are faced with a situation where we cannot find any meaning or purpose, we become aware of the inherent absurdity of existence. This awareness can be frightening, but it also opens up the possibility for radical freedom.
3. Friedrich Nietzsche - Nietzsche was a philosopher who rejected traditional morality and values, and argued that we should create our own values instead. He believed that the experience of nothingness is necessary in order to create new values. He argued that we should embrace the void left by the death of God (i.e., the idea that there is no divine purpose or meaning to life) and use it as a starting point for

creating our own values.

4. Emmanuel Levinas - Levinas was a philosopher who believed that the experience of nothingness is not just a personal or individual experience, but is also a social and ethical one. He argued that we are responsible for the other person and that we must always act ethically towards them. This responsibility arises from the experience of the "face" of the other person, which is a unique and irreducible expression of their individuality.

Overall, the concept of nothingness has been explored in various ways by contemporary Western philosophers, and has been seen as a fundamental aspect of human existence, a source of freedom and creativity, and a social and ethical responsibility.

Nothingness and Modern Western Philosophers

In modern Western philosophy, the concept of nothingness has been explored extensively, especially in the context of existentialism and postmodernism. Here are some key ideas from influential modern philosophers:

1. Maurice Merleau-Ponty - Merleau-Ponty was a phenomenologist who believed that the experience of nothingness is closely tied to the body. He argued that the body is the primary source of our understanding of the world and that the experience of nothingness arises when the body encounters a limit or boundary that cannot be overcome.
2. Jacques Derrida - Derrida was a major figure in postmodern philosophy and believed that the concept of nothingness is closely tied to the idea of deconstruction. He argued that language and meaning are always subject to interpretation and that there is no fixed or stable meaning to anything. This leads to a kind of "nothingness" at the heart of language and meaning.

Overall, the concept of nothingness has been explored in various ways by modern Western philosophers, and has been seen as a fundamental aspect of human existence, a source of anxiety and dread, a necessary condition for creating meaning and values, and a key aspect of language and meaning.

Nothingness and Postmodern Western Philosophers

Postmodern Western philosophers have also explored the concept of nothingness, often in the context of deconstruction and the destabilization of traditional forms of knowledge and meaning. Here are some key ideas from influential postmodern philosophers:

1. Jean-Francois Lyotard - Lyotard argued that the postmodern condition is characterized by a skepticism towards grand narratives or totalizing theories that attempt to explain the world. He saw nothingness as a way to resist the imposition of such narratives and instead embrace the fragmented and contingent nature of reality.
2. Gilles Deleuze - Deleuze believed that nothingness is a positive force that allows for the creation of new possibilities and alternatives. He argued that the task of philosophy is to create concepts that can capture the fluid and dynamic nature of reality, rather than trying to impose fixed categories or meanings.
3. Michel Foucault - Foucault was interested in the ways that power operates in society and how it produces forms of knowledge and subjectivity. He saw nothingness as a way to challenge the authority of traditional forms of knowledge and to create spaces for resistance and alternative modes of being.
4. Judith Butler - Butler's work focuses on the construction of gender and sexuality, and she sees nothingness as a way to disrupt traditional gender norms and identities. She argues that by recognizing the contingency and fluidity of gender, we can create new possibilities for self-expression and community.

Overall, postmodern Western philosophers have used the concept of nothingness as a way to challenge traditional forms of knowledge and meaning, and to create spaces for alternative possibilities and modes of being. They see nothingness as a positive force that allows for the creation of new ideas and perspectives, rather than a source of anxiety or dread.

EASTERN

Nothingness and Ancient Eastern Philosophers

The concept of nothingness has been explored extensively in ancient Eastern philosophy, particularly in the traditions of Taoism, Buddhism, and Hinduism. Here are some key ideas from influential ancient Eastern philosophers:

1. Lao Tzu - Lao Tzu was a Taoist philosopher who believed in the concept of "wu wei," or non-action. He saw nothingness as a way to cultivate

inner stillness and harmony with the natural world. By letting go of attachment to material things and desires, one can achieve a state of nothingness that allows for greater clarity and insight.

2. Buddha - The Buddha taught that the ultimate goal of spiritual practice is to attain enlightenment, which involves transcending the illusions of the ego and realizing the impermanence and emptiness of all things. He taught that clinging to attachments and desires creates suffering and that the realization of nothingness or emptiness is necessary for liberation.
3. Nagarjuna - Nagarjuna was a Buddhist philosopher who developed the concept of "shunyata," or emptiness. He argued that all phenomena are empty of inherent existence and that the realization of this emptiness is essential for attaining enlightenment. By letting go of attachment to fixed ideas and concepts, one can see the world more clearly and achieve greater wisdom and compassion.
4. Zhuangzi - Zhuangzi was a Taoist philosopher who believed in the importance of cultivating a sense of detachment and non-attachment to the world. He saw nothingness as a way to free oneself from the illusions of the ego and to embrace the natural flow of existence.
5. Advaita Vedanta - Advaita Vedanta is a Hindu philosophy that teaches the concept of "Brahman," or the ultimate reality that underlies all existence. The realization of this ultimate reality involves transcending the illusions of the ego and realizing the unity of all things. This involves letting go of attachments and desires and embracing a sense of nothingness or emptiness.

Overall, the concept of nothingness has played a significant role in ancient Eastern philosophy, with many philosophers seeing it as a way to cultivate inner peace, transcend the illusions of the ego, and achieve spiritual liberation.

Nothingness and Medieval Eastern Philosophers

The concept of nothingness continued to be explored in medieval Eastern philosophy, particularly in the traditions of Taoism, Buddhism, and Sufism. Here are some key ideas from influential medieval Eastern philosophers:

1. Ibn Arabi - Ibn Arabi was a Sufi philosopher who believed in the importance of realizing the unity of all things. He saw nothingness as a

way to transcend the illusions of the ego and to achieve a state of unity with the divine. By letting go of attachments and desires, one can attain a state of nothingness that allows for a deeper connection with the divine.

2. Rumi - Rumi was a Sufi poet and philosopher who emphasized the importance of love and connection. He saw nothingness as a way to transcend the ego and to embrace the unity of all things. By letting go of the illusion of separation and embracing a sense of nothingness, one can connect more deeply with others and with the divine.
3. Dogen - Dogen was a Zen Buddhist philosopher who emphasized the importance of meditation and mindfulness. He saw nothingness as a way to cultivate a sense of non-dual awareness and to realize the emptiness of all things. By letting go of attachment to fixed ideas and concepts, one can achieve a state of nothingness that allows for a deeper sense of awareness and understanding.
4. Wang Yangming - Wang Yangming was a Neo-Confucian philosopher who believed in the importance of cultivating moral character. He saw nothingness as a way to cultivate a sense of humility and to let go of the ego's attachment to fixed ideas and concepts. By embracing a sense of nothingness, one can cultivate a more open and receptive attitude towards others and towards the world.

Overall, medieval Eastern philosophers continued to explore the concept of nothingness, seeing it as a way to transcend the illusions of the ego, cultivate inner peace, and connect more deeply with others and with the divine. They emphasized the importance of letting go of attachment to fixed ideas and concepts in order to achieve a deeper sense of awareness and understanding.

Nothingness and Contemporary Eastern Philosophers

The concept of nothingness continues to be explored in contemporary Eastern philosophy, particularly in the traditions of Taoism, Buddhism, and Advaita Vedanta. Here are some key ideas from influential contemporary Eastern philosophers:

1. Thich Nhat Hanh - Thich Nhat Hanh is a Vietnamese Zen master and Buddhist monk who emphasizes the importance of mindfulness and compassion. He sees nothingness as a way to let go of the past and the future and to embrace the present moment fully. By cultivating a sense of nothingness, one can achieve a deeper sense of peace and connectedness

with others and with the world.

2. Dalai Lama - The Dalai Lama is a Tibetan Buddhist leader who emphasizes the importance of compassion and inner peace. He sees nothingness as a way to cultivate a sense of detachment from material possessions and desires, which can lead to greater happiness and inner peace. By embracing a sense of nothingness, one can cultivate greater wisdom and compassion towards oneself and others.
3. Shunryu Suzuki - Shunryu Suzuki was a Japanese Zen master who emphasized the importance of zazen, or seated meditation. He saw nothingness as a way to cultivate a sense of non-dual awareness and to let go of the ego's attachment to fixed ideas and concepts. By embracing a sense of nothingness, one can achieve a deeper sense of inner peace and clarity.
4. Jiddu Krishnamurti - Jiddu Krishnamurti was an Indian philosopher who emphasized the importance of self-inquiry and self-awareness. He saw nothingness as a way to let go of the ego's attachment to the past and the future and to live fully in the present moment. By embracing a sense of nothingness, one can achieve a deeper sense of inner freedom and authenticity.

Overall, contemporary Eastern philosophers continue to explore the concept of nothingness, seeing it as a way to cultivate inner peace, wisdom, and compassion. They emphasize the importance of letting go of attachment to material possessions and desires and embracing a sense of non-dual awareness in order to achieve a deeper sense of inner freedom and authenticity.

Nothingness and Modern Eastern Philosophers

Modern Eastern philosophers continue to explore the concept of nothingness, particularly in the traditions of Taoism, Buddhism, and Advaita Vedanta. Here are some key ideas from influential modern Eastern philosophers:

1. Nishida Kitaro - Nishida Kitaro was a Japanese philosopher who emphasized the importance of intuition and self-awareness. He saw nothingness as a way to transcend the limitations of the ego and to achieve a deeper sense of self-awareness. By embracing a sense of nothingness, one can achieve a state of non-dual awareness and realize the unity of all things.

2. D.T. Suzuki - D.T. Suzuki was a Japanese philosopher who helped to popularize Zen Buddhism in the West. He saw nothingness as a way to cultivate a sense of non-dual awareness and to let go of the ego's attachment to fixed ideas and concepts. By embracing a sense of nothingness, one can achieve a deeper sense of inner peace and clarity.

Overall, modern Eastern philosophers continue to explore the concept of nothingness, seeing it as a way to cultivate inner peace, wisdom, and compassion. They emphasize the importance of letting go of attachment to fixed ideas and concepts, and embracing a sense of non-dual awareness in order to achieve a deeper sense of self-awareness, inner freedom, and authenticity.

Nothingness and Postmodern Eastern Philosophers

Postmodern Eastern philosophers have continued to explore the concept of nothingness, particularly in the traditions of Taoism, Buddhism, and Advaita Vedanta. Here are some key ideas from influential postmodern Eastern philosophers:

1. Keiji Nishitani - Keiji Nishitani was a Japanese philosopher who combined elements of Zen Buddhism and existentialism in his work. He saw nothingness as a fundamental aspect of human existence and emphasized the importance of accepting the reality of nothingness in order to live a meaningful life. By embracing nothingness, one can cultivate a sense of gratitude and awe for the world as it is.
2. Yuasa Yasuo - Yuasa Yasuo was a Japanese philosopher who emphasized the importance of embodied experience and the relationship between self and world. He saw nothingness as a way to open up the self to the world and to cultivate a sense of interconnectedness with all beings. By embracing a sense of nothingness, one can achieve a state of non-dual awareness and realize the interdependent nature of all things.
3. Ken Wilber - Ken Wilber is an American philosopher who has drawn on various Eastern and Western traditions in his work. He sees nothingness as a way to transcend the limitations of the ego and to achieve a state of non-dual awareness. By embracing a sense of nothingness, one can realize the unity of all things and cultivate a sense of compassion and interconnectedness with all beings.
4. Deepak Chopra - Deepak Chopra is an Indian-American author and spiritual teacher who draws on various Eastern and Western traditions

in his work. He sees nothingness as a way to cultivate a sense of inner peace and harmony. By embracing a sense of nothingness, one can let go of attachment to the past and the future and fully embrace the present moment.

Overall, postmodern Eastern philosophers continue to explore the concept of nothingness, seeing it as a fundamental aspect of human existence and a way to cultivate inner peace, wisdom, and interconnectedness with all beings. They emphasize the importance of accepting the reality of nothingness and letting go of attachment to fixed ideas and concepts in order to live a meaningful and fulfilling life.

TWO

NOTHINGNESS AND ISM

The concept of nothingness has continued to be relevant in contemporary thought, particularly in the fields of philosophy and physics. In philosophy, the concept of nothingness has been explored in relation to questions of existence, meaning, and the nature of reality. Many contemporary philosophers have explored the concept of nothingness through various approaches, including phenomenology, existentialism, and postmodernism.

Nothingness and Phenomenologism

In phenomenology, the concept of nothingness is related to the idea of "the nothing," which refers to the absence of any particular object or content of consciousness. The nothing is not a particular thing, but rather a fundamental aspect of human experience that allows for the possibility of meaningful experience and perception.

According to phenomenological philosopher Martin Heidegger, the nothing is not simply a lack of objects or content, but is instead a fundamental aspect of the way that humans experience the world. He argues that the nothing is a necessary part of human existence, and is the source of the possibility for meaningful experience and perception.

In phenomenological practice, the concept of nothingness is related to the idea of "bracketing," or the process of setting aside assumptions and preconceptions in order to focus on the pure experience of a particular phenomenon. By bracketing off assumptions and focusing on the pure experience, the individual can become aware of the nothing as a fundamental aspect of human experience.

Overall, the concept of nothingness in phenomenology can be seen as a way of acknowledging the fundamental absence that is necessary for meaningful experience and perception. It is a key concept in phenomenological philosophy and practice, and has inspired many to seek a deeper understanding of the nature of human consciousness and experience.

Nothingness and Existentialism

In existentialism, the concept of nothingness is related to the idea of human freedom and responsibility. According to this view, humans are faced with the possibility of nothingness, or the absence of inherent meaning or purpose in the universe. This realization can lead to feelings of anxiety, despair, and alienation, but it can also inspire individuals to create their own meaning and values in a world without inherent meaning.

Existentialist philosopher Jean-Paul Sartre argues that nothingness is a fundamental aspect of human existence. He claims that humans are condemned to be free, meaning that they must create their own values and meanings in a world without inherent meaning or purpose. This freedom can be a source of anxiety and despair, but it can also lead to a sense of authentic existence and the possibility of creating one's own destiny.

Existentialist philosophers also argue that the awareness of nothingness can lead to a sense of radical responsibility. In a world without inherent meaning or purpose, individuals are responsible for creating their own values and meanings, and for taking responsibility for their own lives and actions.

Overall, the concept of nothingness in existentialism can be seen as a way of acknowledging the absence of inherent meaning or purpose in the universe, and the responsibility that comes with creating one's own values and meanings. It is a key concept in existentialist philosophy and has inspired many to seek a deeper understanding of the nature of human existence and the path to a meaningful life.

Nothingness and Modernism

In modernism, the concept of nothingness can be seen as a reaction against traditional forms and values in art and literature. Modernist artists and writers sought to break away from the conventions of the past and create new forms of expression that reflected the modern world.

One way that the concept of nothingness is expressed in modernist art and literature is through the use of fragmentation and abstraction. Modernist works often break down traditional forms and structures, leaving empty spaces or gaps that invite the viewer or reader to fill in the missing pieces.

Another way that the concept of nothingness is expressed in modernism is through the use of irony and satire. Modernist artists and writers often use humor and irony to critique traditional values and beliefs, creating a sense of nothingness or emptiness in the face of established cultural norms.

In some modernist works, the concept of nothingness is expressed through a sense of alienation and despair. Modernist writers and artists often depict characters or situations that are isolated or disconnected from the larger society, creating a sense of meaninglessness and emptiness.

Overall, the concept of nothingness in modernism can be seen as a way of challenging traditional forms and values, and of creating new forms of expression that reflect the fragmented and uncertain nature of the modern world. It has inspired many artists and writers to explore new ways of creating meaning and value in the face of the emptiness and chaos of the modern age.

Nothingness and Idealism

The concept of nothingness has been explored in various philosophical traditions, including idealism. In idealism, the emphasis is placed on the primacy of ideas or the mind, rather than the material world.

In the idealist view, nothingness is not simply an absence of things, but rather a condition of possibility for the manifestation of things. One way that nothingness has been incorporated into idealist thought is through the idea of negative or privative concepts. This is because, in the idealist perspective, the material world is not the ultimate reality, but rather a product of the mind or spirit. For example, the German philosopher Georg Wilhelm Friedrich Hegel argued that nothingness is an essential aspect of the dialectical process by which reality unfolds. In Hegelian philosophy, nothingness is not simply an absence of being, but rather a moment of negation that drives the process of becoming and transformation.

Similarly, the philosopher Immanuel Kant used the concept of nothingness in his arguments about the limits of human knowledge. According to Kant, the human mind can never know the "thing-in-itself," or the ultimate reality that exists beyond our perceptions. This concept of the unknowable or the negative is a central component of Kant's idealist philosophy.

In addition, some forms of idealism, such as the philosophy of Absolute Idealism, posit the existence of an all-encompassing consciousness or spirit that underlies all reality. In this view, nothingness is not an absence or a void, but rather a necessary aspect of the creative process by which the Absolute generates new ideas and realities.

Overall, the relationship between nothingness and idealism is complex and multifaceted, and has been explored in various ways by different philosophers and traditions.

Nothingness and Rationalism

Rationalism is a philosophical approach that emphasizes reason and logic as the primary sources of knowledge and truth. In the context of nothingness, rationalist philosophers have often approached the concept in a more analytical and logical way, seeking to understand it through reason and deduction. Here are some key ideas from rationalist philosophers on nothingness:

1. René Descartes - René Descartes was a French philosopher who is often considered the father of modern rationalism. He saw nothingness as a kind of absence, or the lack of existence. For Descartes, the concept of nothingness was important in his quest for certainty and knowledge, as it helped him to distinguish between what he knew for sure and what was uncertain or false.
2. Gottfried Wilhelm Leibniz - Gottfried Wilhelm Leibniz was a German philosopher and mathematician who developed the concept of monads, which are individual, self-contained units of reality. He saw nothingness as a kind of impossibility, as the very concept of nothingness implies the absence of any kind of entity or thing, which contradicts the idea of monads.
3. Immanuel Kant - Immanuel Kant was a German philosopher who developed a complex system of ethics and metaphysics based on reason and logic. He saw nothingness as a kind of limit to human understanding, beyond which reason and logic cannot penetrate. For Kant, the concept of nothingness was important in understanding the limitations of human knowledge and the need for humility and skepticism.
4. Bertrand Russell - Bertrand Russell was a British philosopher and logician who developed the theory of logical atomism, which holds that the world can be understood as a series of atomic facts that can be analyzed logically. He saw nothingness as a kind of absence or negation, which could be understood through logical analysis. For Russell, the

concept of nothingness was important in understanding the nature of reality and the limits of human knowledge.

Overall, rationalist philosophers have approached the concept of nothingness through reason and logic, seeking to understand it as a kind of absence or negation that can be analyzed and understood through analytical methods. They have emphasized the importance of nothingness in understanding the nature of reality and the limits of human knowledge, and have often used it as a tool for philosophical inquiry and investigation.

Nothingness and Romanticism

Romanticism is a cultural movement that emerged in the late 18th century and emphasized emotional expression, imagination, and the individual experience. In the context of nothingness, Romantic philosophers often approached the concept in a more intuitive and emotional way, seeking to understand it through subjective experience and feeling. Here are some key ideas from Romantic philosophers on nothingness:

1. William Wordsworth - William Wordsworth was an English poet who emphasized the importance of nature and the individual experience in his work. He saw nothingness as a kind of emptiness or void that could be filled with the beauty and wonder of the natural world. For Wordsworth, the experience of nothingness was often a prelude to a spiritual awakening or a moment of profound insight.
2. Samuel Taylor Coleridge - Samuel Taylor Coleridge was an English poet and philosopher who developed the concept of the "willing suspension of disbelief," which is the idea that the audience of a work of fiction must be willing to set aside their disbelief in order to fully engage with the story. He saw nothingness as a kind of threshold between the world of reality and the world of imagination, and emphasized the importance of crossing that threshold in order to fully engage with the world of art and creativity.
3. Søren Kierkegaard - Søren Kierkegaard was a Danish philosopher who emphasized the importance of subjective experience and the individual's relationship to God in his work. He saw nothingness as a kind of existential dread or anxiety that could only be overcome through a leap of faith and a surrender of the self to God. For Kierkegaard, the experience of nothingness was often a prelude to a moment of spiritual

awakening or a realization of one's own limitations and dependence on a higher power.

Overall, Romantic philosophers approached the concept of nothingness through intuition and feeling, seeking to understand it as a threshold between the world of reality and the world of imagination, or as a void that could be filled with the creative power of the individual will. They emphasized the importance of subjective experience and the individual's relationship to the natural world, the world of art and creativity, or to a higher power.

Nothingness and Postmodernism

Postmodernism is a cultural movement that emerged in the mid-20th century and challenged the modernist view of progress, rationality, and objective truth. In the context of nothingness, postmodern philosophers often approached the concept in a more critical and deconstructive way, seeking to expose the ways in which it has been used to maintain power and control. Here are some key ideas from postmodern philosophers on nothingness:

1. Jacques Derrida - Jacques Derrida was a French philosopher who developed the concept of deconstruction, which is a method of analyzing texts and ideas by exposing their internal contradictions and assumptions. He saw nothingness as a kind of absence or lack that is always present within language and thought, and emphasized the importance of recognizing this absence in order to deconstruct the dominant discourses that shape our world.
2. Jean Baudrillard - Jean Baudrillard was a French philosopher who developed the concept of simulation, which is the idea that our world is increasingly mediated by images and signs that have no connection to any underlying reality. He saw nothingness as a kind of simulation, or a hyperreal void that is created by our own efforts to simulate reality through language and media.
3. Michel Foucault - Michel Foucault was a French philosopher who developed the concept of power/knowledge, which is the idea that knowledge and power are inextricably linked and that dominant discourses are used to maintain power and control. He saw nothingness as a kind of limit or boundary that is imposed by these discourses, and emphasized the importance of challenging these boundaries in order to

create new possibilities for thought and action.

4. Gilles Deleuze - Gilles Deleuze was a French philosopher who developed the concept of the virtual, which is the idea that there are infinite possibilities for thought and action that are not yet actualized in the world. He saw nothingness as a kind of virtual space that is filled with these possibilities, and emphasized the importance of exploring this space in order to create new ways of thinking and being in the world.

Overall, postmodern philosophers approached the concept of nothingness in a critical and deconstructive way, seeking to expose the ways in which it has been used to maintain power and control. They emphasized the importance of recognizing the limits and boundaries that are imposed by dominant discourses, and of exploring the virtual space of possibilities that is opened up by the recognition of these limits.

Nothingness and Aestheticism

The concept of "nothingness" has been explored in various fields of study, including philosophy, physics, and psychology. In aesthetics, "nothingness" is often used to refer to the absence of visual or auditory stimuli in a work of art.

Some artists and philosophers have argued that nothingness can be an essential element of aesthetic experience. For example, the Japanese concept of "ma" (literally meaning "gap" or "pause") emphasizes the importance of empty spaces or moments of silence in art, music, and other forms of expression. Similarly, the French philosopher Maurice Merleau-Ponty argued that negative space (the space between and around objects) is just as important as positive space in shaping our perception of a work of art.

In some artistic movements, such as minimalism, the use of negative space or emptiness is deliberately incorporated into the artwork to create a sense of simplicity and clarity. For example, the artist Agnes Martin created minimalist paintings that emphasized the use of white space and subtle grids to evoke a sense of calmness and serenity.

In contrast, other artists and thinkers have argued that nothingness is a void that cannot be filled by aesthetic experience. The Russian philosopher Nikolai Berdyaev, for example, argued that art is incapable of fully capturing the transcendent or spiritual aspects of human experience.

Ultimately, the relationship between nothingness and aesthetic experience is a complex and multifaceted one, and different artists and philosophers have approached the topic in different ways.

Nothingness and Atheistism

In atheistic philosophy, the concept of nothingness can be seen as a rejection of the idea of a supernatural or transcendent reality. Atheists generally do not believe in the existence of a God or gods, and therefore do not see nothingness as related to any divine or spiritual realm.

Instead, the concept of nothingness in atheistic philosophy can be seen as a way of acknowledging the limitations of human understanding and the ultimate reality of the natural world. Atheists may view nothingness as a natural state that exists when there is a lack of physical or material objects, rather than a spiritual or transcendent state.

In some schools of existentialist philosophy, the concept of nothingness is related to the idea of human freedom and responsibility. According to this view, humans are faced with the possibility of nothingness, or the absence of meaning or purpose, and must create their own meaning and values in a world without inherent meaning.

Overall, the concept of nothingness in atheistic philosophy can be seen as a way of acknowledging the limitations of human understanding and the ultimate reality of the natural world. It is a fundamental aspect of atheist thought, and has inspired many to seek a deeper understanding of the nature of existence and the path to a meaningful life.

THREE

NOTHINGNESS AND CONCEPTS

Nothingness and Being

Nothingness and being are concepts that have been explored in various fields of philosophy, including metaphysics, existentialism, and ontology.

In metaphysics, being refers to the existence of things in the world, while nothingness refers to the absence of existence. Some philosophers argue that nothingness does not truly exist, as even when we think of something as "non-existent," we are still referring to it in some way.

In existentialism, being refers to the individual's experience of existence, and the search for meaning in life. Nothingness is often seen as the underlying emptiness or lack of meaning that individuals may feel, which can lead to feelings of anxiety and despair.

In ontology, being refers to the nature of existence itself, and the study of what exists and how it exists. Nothingness is often seen as the absence of being, or the lack of any existence at all.

Overall, the concepts of nothingness and being are complex and multifaceted, and have been explored in various philosophical traditions throughout history.

Nothingness and Doing

The concepts of nothingness and doing are also intertwined in philosophy, particularly in the context of existentialism and the search for meaning in life.

In existentialism, nothingness is often seen as the underlying emptiness or lack of meaning that individuals may feel in their lives. This sense of nothingness can lead to feelings of despair and anxiety, as individuals struggle to find purpose and significance in their existence.

One way to combat this sense of nothingness is through action or doing. Existentialist philosophers often emphasize the importance of taking responsibility for one's own life and actively creating meaning through actions and choices.

In this sense, doing can be seen as a way of filling the void of nothingness and creating purpose and significance in life. By taking action and making choices, individuals can create their own sense of meaning and overcome the existential despair that can come with a sense of nothingness.

However, it is important to note that not all actions are equally meaningful, and the search for purpose and significance in life can be a lifelong journey. The relationship between nothingness and doing is complex and multifaceted, and has been explored by many philosophers throughout history.

Nothingness and Having

The concepts of nothingness and having are also intertwined in philosophy, particularly in the context of material possessions and their relationship to happiness and fulfilment.

In some philosophical traditions, such as Buddhism, the pursuit of material possessions is seen as a source of suffering and dissatisfaction. The idea is that attachments to material possessions can lead to a sense of emptiness or nothingness, as individuals are always searching for the next thing to acquire or possess.

On the other hand, some philosophical traditions emphasize the importance of having material possessions as a means of fulfilling basic needs and achieving a sense of security and comfort in life. The relationship between having and nothingness is complex and multifaceted, and depends on one's personal beliefs and values.

Ultimately, the pursuit of material possessions can never fully fill the void of nothingness or provide a sense of lasting happiness or fulfilment. Some philosophers argue that true fulfilment can only be achieved through the cultivation of inner virtues and the pursuit of higher values, such as love, compassion, and wisdom.

Nothingness and Existence

The concepts of nothingness and existence are fundamental to many philosophical traditions, particularly in the realm of metaphysics and ontology.

In metaphysics, existence is often seen as a fundamental characteristic of being, while nothingness is the absence of existence. However, some philosophers argue that nothingness is not a positive existence in itself, but rather a negation of existence.

In ontology, the study of existence itself, the relationship between nothingness and existence is complex and multifaceted. Some philosophers argue that nothingness is a necessary condition for the existence of things, as without nothingness, there would be no distinction between things that exist and things that do not.

Existentialist philosophy also explores the relationship between nothingness and existence, particularly in the context of the human experience of being-in-the-world. Existentialists often emphasize the human capacity for freedom and choice, which can create a sense of nothingness or existential angst in the face of the vastness and uncertainty of existence.

Overall, the relationship between nothingness and existence is a rich and complex philosophical topic that has been explored by many thinkers throughout history.

Nothingness and Transcendence

The concepts of nothingness and transcendence are often explored in the context of existentialism and spirituality.

In existentialism, nothingness refers to the underlying emptiness or lack of meaning that individuals may feel in their lives. This sense of nothingness can lead to feelings of despair and anxiety, as individuals struggle to find purpose and significance in their existence. Transcendence, on the other hand, refers to the idea of going beyond oneself and connecting with something greater, such as a higher power, nature, or humanity as a whole.

For some existentialist philosophers, transcendence is seen as a way of overcoming the sense of nothingness and finding meaning and purpose in life. By connecting with something greater than oneself, individuals can transcend their individual concerns and find a sense of fulfilment and purpose.

In spiritual traditions, transcendence often refers to the experience of going beyond the limitations of the physical world and connecting with a higher spiritual reality. Some spiritual traditions, such as Buddhism, see the pursuit of transcendence as a way of overcoming the suffering that arises from attachment to material possessions and the sense of self.

The relationship between nothingness and transcendence is complex and multifaceted, and has been explored by many philosophers and spiritual leaders throughout history. Ultimately, the pursuit of transcendence can be seen as a way of overcoming the sense of nothingness and finding a deeper sense of meaning and purpose in life

Nothingness and Freedom

The concepts of nothingness and freedom are often explored in philosophy, particularly in the context of existentialism and the human experience of freedom.

In existentialism, nothingness often refers to the underlying emptiness or lack of meaning that individuals may feel in their lives. This sense of nothingness can lead to feelings of despair and anxiety, as individuals struggle to find purpose and significance in their existence.

However, some existentialist philosophers argue that nothingness can also be a source of freedom. By recognizing the inherent emptiness and lack of meaning in existence, individuals can liberate themselves from social and cultural expectations and create their own meaning and purpose.

Freedom is often seen as a key aspect of the human experience in existentialism, as individuals are seen as free to create their own values and meanings in life. The sense of nothingness can be seen as a necessary condition for this freedom, as it allows individuals to break free from preconceived notions of what is important or valuable in life.

However, the relationship between nothingness and freedom is complex and multifaceted. Some philosophers argue that too much focus on freedom can lead to a sense of nihilism or emptiness, as individuals become disconnected from a sense of community or shared values. Others argue that freedom must be balanced with responsibility and consideration for others in order to create a meaningful and fulfilling life.

Overall, the relationship between nothingness and freedom is a rich and complex philosophical topic that has been explored by many thinkers throughout history.

Nothingness and Will

The concepts of nothingness and will are often explored in philosophy, particularly in the context of existentialism and the human experience of agency.

In existentialism, nothingness often refers to the underlying emptiness or lack of meaning that individuals may feel in their lives. This sense of nothingness can lead to feelings of despair and anxiety, as individuals struggle to find purpose and significance in their existence.

However, some existentialist philosophers argue that nothingness can also be a source of will. By recognizing the inherent emptiness and lack of meaning in existence, individuals can become more aware of their own agency and ability to create meaning in their lives.

Will is often seen as a key aspect of the human experience in existentialism, as individuals are seen as free to create their own values and meanings in life. The sense of nothingness can be seen as a necessary condition for this will, as it allows individuals to break free from preconceived notions of what is important or valuable in life and create their own path.

However, the relationship between nothingness and will is complex and multifaceted. Some philosophers argue that too much focus on will can lead to a sense of arrogance or self-centeredness, as individuals become too focused on their own goals and desires. Others argue that will must be balanced with acceptance and humility in order to create a meaningful and fulfilling life.

Overall, the relationship between nothingness and will is a rich and complex philosophical topic that has been explored by many thinkers throughout history.

Nothingness and Intellect

The concepts of nothingness and intellect are often explored in philosophy, particularly in the context of epistemology and the nature of knowledge.

In epistemology, the study of knowledge itself, the relationship between nothingness and intellect is complex and multifaceted. Some philosophers argue that nothingness is a necessary condition for the existence of knowledge, as without nothingness, there would be no distinction between things that exist and things that do not. This distinction is fundamental to the process of acquiring knowledge and understanding the world around us.

Others argue that the pursuit of knowledge can lead to a sense of nothingness, as the more we learn about the world, the more we become aware of how much we do not know. This sense of nothingness can be seen as a source of humility and openness to new perspectives, but it can also lead to feelings of despair and nihilism.

In terms of intellect, some philosophers argue that the pursuit of knowledge and understanding is a key aspect of the human experience, and that the development of our intellectual abilities is what sets us apart from other animals. However, others argue that too much focus on intellect can lead to a sense of alienation from our emotions and our sense of humanity.

Overall, the relationship between nothingness and intellect is a rich and complex philosophical topic that has been explored by many thinkers throughout history. The pursuit of knowledge and understanding can be seen as a way of transcending our sense of nothingness and finding meaning and purpose in the world, but it must be balanced with humility and an appreciation of our emotional and spiritual dimensions.

Nothingness and Facticity

The concepts of nothingness and facticity are often explored in philosophy, particularly in the context of existentialism and the human experience of being in the world.

In existentialism, facticity refers to the concrete and unalterable aspects of our existence, such as our biological makeup, our cultural and social backgrounds, and the historical and political context in which we live. These factors shape who we are and the possibilities available to us in life.

Nothingness, on the other hand, refers to the underlying emptiness or lack of meaning that individuals may feel in their lives. This sense of nothingness can lead to feelings of despair and anxiety, as individuals struggle to find purpose and significance in their existence.

However, some existentialist philosophers argue that nothingness and facticity are intertwined, and that it is through the recognition of our facticity that we can transcend our sense of nothingness and find meaning and purpose in life. By acknowledging the limitations and constraints of our existence, we can better understand ourselves and the world around us, and make choices that are authentic and meaningful.

The relationship between nothingness and facticity is complex and multifaceted. Some philosophers argue that too much focus on facticity can lead to a sense of determinism or fatalism, as individuals become too focused on the limitations and constraints of their existence. Others argue that nothingness must be balanced with an awareness of our facticity in order to create a meaningful and fulfilling life.

Overall, the relationship between nothingness and facticity is a rich and complex philosophical topic that has been explored by many thinkers throughout history. The recognition of our facticity can be seen as a way of transcending our sense of nothingness and finding meaning and purpose in the world, but it must be balanced with an appreciation of our freedom and agency as individuals.

Nothingness and Temporality

The concepts of nothingness and temporality are often explored in philosophy, particularly in the context of existentialism and the human experience of time.

In existentialism, nothingness often refers to the underlying emptiness or lack of meaning that individuals may feel in their lives. This sense of nothingness can lead to feelings of despair and anxiety, as individuals struggle to find purpose and significance in their existence.

Temporality, on the other hand, refers to the experience of time and the way it structures our lives. The past, present, and future are seen as interconnected and interdependent, shaping who we are and the possibilities available to us in life.

Some existentialist philosophers argue that the relationship between nothingness and temporality is fundamental to the human experience. By recognizing the transience and impermanence of our existence, we can better appreciate the present moment and find meaning and purpose in life. The past and future are seen as sources of possibility and potential, rather than as constraints on our existence.

However, the relationship between nothingness and temporality is complex and multifaceted. Some philosophers argue that too much focus on the present moment can lead to a sense of detachment from the past and future, and a lack of appreciation for the broader context of our existence. Others argue that an excessive focus on the past and future can lead to a sense of nostalgia or anxiety, as individuals struggle to come to terms with the impermanence of their existence.

Overall, the relationship between nothingness and temporality is a rich and complex philosophical topic that has been explored by many thinkers throughout history. The recognition of the impermanence and transience of our existence can be seen as a way of transcending our sense of nothingness and finding meaning and purpose in the world, but it must be balanced with an appreciation of the broader context of our existence and the possibilities available to us in life.

Nothingness and Origin

The concepts of nothingness and origin are often explored in philosophy, particularly in the context of existentialism and the human experience of being in the world.

In existentialism, nothingness often refers to the underlying emptiness or lack of meaning that individuals may feel in their lives. This sense of nothingness can lead to feelings of despair and anxiety, as individuals struggle to find purpose and significance in their existence.

Origin, on the other hand, refers to the idea of where we come from and the factors that shape our identity. This can include biological factors, cultural and social backgrounds, and historical and political contexts.

Some existentialist philosophers argue that the relationship between nothingness and origin is fundamental to the human experience. By recognizing the contingency and unpredictability of our origin, we can better appreciate the unique aspects of our identity and find meaning and purpose in life. Rather than seeing our origin as a fixed and determinate aspect of our existence, we can see it as a source of possibility and potential.

However, the relationship between nothingness and origin is complex and multifaceted. Some philosophers argue that too much focus on the contingency and unpredictability of our origin can lead to a sense of rootlessness or disconnection from our past and cultural heritage. Others argue that an excessive focus on the past can lead to a sense of nostalgia or sentimentality, as individuals struggle to come to terms with the impermanence of their existence.

Overall, the relationship between nothingness and origin is a rich and complex philosophical topic that has been explored by many thinkers throughout history. The recognition of the contingency and unpredictability of our origin can be seen as a way of transcending our sense of nothingness and finding meaning and purpose in the world, but it must be balanced with an appreciation of the unique aspects of our identity and the broader context of our existence.

Nothingness and Time

The relationship between nothingness and time is a fundamental and complex philosophical topic that has been explored by many thinkers throughout history, particularly in the context of existentialism.

In existentialism, nothingness often refers to the underlying emptiness or lack of meaning that individuals may feel in their lives. This sense of nothingness can lead to feelings of despair and anxiety, as individuals struggle to find purpose and significance in their existence.

Time, on the other hand, refers to the experience of the passage of time and the way it structures our lives. The past, present, and future are seen as interconnected and interdependent, shaping who we are and the possibilities available to us in life.

Some philosophers argue that the relationship between nothingness and time is fundamental to the human experience. By recognizing the transience and impermanence of our existence, we can better appreciate the present moment and find meaning and purpose in life. The past and future are seen as sources of possibility and potential, rather than as constraints on our existence.

However, the relationship between nothingness and time is complex and multifaceted. Some philosophers argue that too much focus on the present moment can lead to a sense of detachment from the past and future, and a lack of appreciation for the broader context of our existence. Others argue that an excessive focus on the past and future can lead to a sense of nostalgia or anxiety, as individuals struggle to come to terms with the impermanence of their existence.

Overall, the relationship between nothingness and time is a rich and complex philosophical topic that has been explored by many thinkers throughout history. The recognition of the impermanence and transience of our existence can be seen as a way of transcending our sense of nothingness and finding meaning and purpose in the world, but it must be balanced with an appreciation of the broader context of our existence and the possibilities available to us in life.

Nothingness and Consciousness

The relationship between nothingness and consciousness is a fundamental and complex philosophical topic that has been explored by many thinkers throughout history.

In existentialism, nothingness often refers to the underlying emptiness or lack of meaning that individuals may feel in their lives. This sense of nothingness can lead to feelings of despair and anxiety, as individuals struggle to find purpose and significance in their existence.

Consciousness, on the other hand, refers to the subjective experience of awareness and the ability to perceive and interact with the world around us. It is often seen as the basis of our sense of self and our ability to make meaning in the world.

Some philosophers argue that the relationship between nothingness and consciousness is fundamental to the human experience. By recognizing the underlying emptiness of existence, individuals can transcend their sense of self and connect with a broader sense of being or consciousness. This can lead to a sense of interconnectedness with the world and a deeper appreciation for the mysteries of existence.

However, the relationship between nothingness and consciousness is complex and multifaceted. Some philosophers argue that too much focus on the emptiness of existence can lead to a sense of nihilism or despair, as individuals struggle to find meaning and purpose in life. Others argue that an excessive focus on consciousness can lead to a sense of detachment from the world, as individuals retreat into their own subjective experiences.

Overall, the relationship between nothingness and consciousness is a rich and complex philosophical topic that has been explored by many thinkers throughout history. The recognition of the underlying emptiness of existence can be seen as a way of transcending our sense of self and connecting with a broader sense of consciousness, but it must be balanced with an appreciation for the meaningfulness of our subjective experiences and the possibilities available to us in life.

Nothingness and Sub-consciousness

The relationship between nothingness and sub-consciousness is a complex and multifaceted philosophical topic that has been explored by many thinkers throughout history.

In existentialism, nothingness often refers to the underlying emptiness or lack of meaning that individuals may feel in their lives. This sense of nothingness can lead to feelings of despair and anxiety, as individuals struggle to find purpose and significance in their existence.

Sub-consciousness, on the other hand, refers to the part of the mind that operates below the level of conscious awareness, influencing our thoughts, feelings, and behaviour. It is often seen as the source of our deepest desires, fears, and motivations.

Some philosophers argue that the relationship between nothingness and sub-consciousness is fundamental to the human experience. By exploring and understanding the deeper layers of our subconscious mind, we can uncover the sources of our sense of nothingness and find new possibilities for growth and transformation.

However, the relationship between nothingness and sub-consciousness is complex and multifaceted. Some philosophers argue that too much focus on the subconscious mind can lead to a sense of detachment from reality, as individuals retreat into their own inner world. Others argue that an excessive focus on the conscious mind can lead to a sense of superficiality or lack of depth, as individuals ignore the deeper layers of their subconscious experience.

Overall, the relationship between nothingness and sub-consciousness is a rich and complex philosophical topic that has been explored by many thinkers throughout history. The recognition of the underlying emptiness of existence can be seen as a way of uncovering the deeper layers of our subconscious mind and finding new possibilities for growth and transformation, but it must be balanced with an appreciation for the meaningfulness of our conscious experiences and the interconnectedness of our existence.

Nothingness and Unconsciousness

The relationship between nothingness and unconsciousness is a complex and multifaceted philosophical topic that has been explored by many thinkers throughout history.

In existentialism, nothingness often refers to the underlying emptiness or lack of meaning that individuals may feel in their lives. This sense of nothingness can lead to feelings of despair and anxiety, as individuals struggle to find purpose and significance in their existence.

Unconsciousness, on the other hand, refers to the state of being unaware or lacking consciousness, such as during sleep or under anaesthesia. It is often seen as the opposite of consciousness and the source of our deepest fears and desires.

Some philosophers argue that the relationship between nothingness and unconsciousness is fundamental to the human experience. By exploring and understanding the deeper layers of our unconscious mind, we can uncover the sources of our sense of nothingness and find new possibilities for growth and transformation.

However, the relationship between nothingness and unconsciousness is complex and multifaceted. Some philosophers argue that too much focus on the unconscious mind can lead to a sense of detachment from reality, as individuals retreat into their own inner world. Others argue that an excessive focus on the conscious mind can lead to a sense of superficiality or lack of depth, as individuals ignore the deeper layers of their unconscious experience.

Overall, the relationship between nothingness and unconsciousness is a rich and complex philosophical topic that has been explored by many thinkers throughout history. The recognition of the underlying emptiness of existence can be seen as a way of uncovering the deeper layers of our unconscious mind and finding new possibilities for growth and transformation, but it must be balanced with an appreciation for the meaningfulness of our conscious experiences and the interconnectedness of our existence.

Nothingness and Self

The relationship between nothingness and self is a complex and multifaceted philosophical topic that has been explored by many thinkers throughout history.

In existentialism, nothingness often refers to the underlying emptiness or lack of meaning that individuals may feel in their lives. This sense of nothingness can lead to feelings of despair and anxiety, as individuals struggle to find purpose and significance in their existence.

The concept of self, on the other hand, refers to the individual's sense of personal identity and subjectivity. It is the sense of "I" that defines our sense of self and distinguishes us from others.

Some philosophers argue that the sense of self is intimately connected to the experience of nothingness. They argue that by recognizing the underlying emptiness of existence, individuals can come to a deeper understanding of themselves and their place in the world. By accepting the limitations of the self and the inherent impermanence of all things, individuals can achieve a greater sense of inner peace and freedom.

However, the relationship between nothingness and self is complex and multifaceted. Some philosophers argue that too much focus on the self can lead to a sense of egocentrism and self-absorption, as individuals become disconnected from the broader context of their existence. Others argue that an excessive focus on nothingness can lead to a sense of nihilism and despair, as individuals lose sight of the meaning and purpose of their lives.

Overall, the relationship between nothingness and self is a rich and complex philosophical topic that has been explored by many thinkers throughout history. The recognition of the underlying emptiness of existence can be seen as a way of deepening our understanding of ourselves and our place in the world, but it must be balanced with an appreciation for the meaningfulness of our conscious experiences and the interconnectedness of our existence.

Nothingness and the Other

The relationship between nothingness and the other is a complex and multifaceted philosophical topic that has been explored by many thinkers throughout history.

In existentialism, nothingness often refers to the underlying emptiness or lack of meaning that individuals may feel in their lives. The other, on the other hand, refers to those who are different from us, who we encounter in the world, and with whom we interact.

Some philosophers argue that the experience of encountering the other can be a way of confronting our own sense of nothingness. By recognizing the fundamental differences between ourselves and others, we can come to a deeper understanding of our own limitations and imperfections. This recognition can lead to a greater sense of empathy and connection with others, as we see ourselves reflected in the experiences of those around us.

However, the relationship between nothingness and the other is complex and multifaceted. Some philosophers argue that too much focus on the other can lead to a sense of alienation and detachment from our own experience. Others argue that an excessive focus on our own sense of nothingness can lead to a sense of isolation and disconnection from others.

Overall, the relationship between nothingness and the other is a rich and complex philosophical topic that has been explored by many thinkers throughout history. The recognition of the fundamental differences between ourselves and others can be seen as a way of deepening our understanding of ourselves and our place in the world, but it must be balanced with an appreciation for the interconnectedness of all things and the need for empathy and connection with others.

Nothingness and the World

The relationship between nothingness and the world is a complex and multifaceted philosophical topic that has been explored by many thinkers throughout history.

In existentialism, nothingness often refers to the underlying emptiness or lack of meaning that individuals may feel in their lives. The world, on the other hand, refers to the totality of all that exists outside of ourselves, including both the physical and social environment in which we live.

Some philosophers argue that the experience of nothingness can lead to a sense of detachment from the world, as individuals struggle to find meaning and purpose in their existence. However, others argue that the recognition of nothingness can actually deepen our appreciation for the world and our place in it. By recognizing the fundamental impermanence of all things, we can come to a greater appreciation for the beauty and value of the world around us.

Similarly, the world can also be seen as a source of meaning and significance in the face of nothingness. By engaging with the world and contributing to the ongoing flow of history and culture, individuals can find purpose and fulfilment in their existence.

Overall, the relationship between nothingness and the world is a rich and complex philosophical topic that has been explored by many thinkers throughout history. The recognition of nothingness can lead to a greater appreciation for the beauty and value of the world around us, but it must be balanced with a recognition of the impermanence of all things and the need to find meaning and purpose in our engagement with the world.

Nothingness and Body

The relationship between nothingness and the body is a complex and multifaceted philosophical topic that has been explored by many thinkers throughout history.

In existentialism, nothingness often refers to the underlying emptiness or lack of meaning that individuals may feel in their lives. The body, on the other hand, refers to the physical manifestation of the self in the world, including our senses, emotions, and bodily experiences.

Some philosophers argue that the body can be a source of meaning and significance in the face of nothingness. By engaging with the world through our physical senses and experiences, we can find pleasure, joy, and a sense of connection with others.

However, others argue that an excessive focus on the body can lead to a sense of detachment from our own sense of nothingness. By focusing too much on our physical experiences, we may lose sight of the deeper existential questions that give our lives meaning and purpose.

Overall, the relationship between nothingness and the body is a rich and complex philosophical topic that has been explored by many thinkers throughout history. While the body can be a source of pleasure and connection, it must be balanced with a recognition of the underlying emptiness that defines the human condition. By acknowledging the impermanence of our physical experiences and the underlying nothingness that defines our existence, we can come to a deeper appreciation for the beauty and value of our embodied experiences in the world.

Nothingness and Limitedness

The relationship between nothingness and limitedness is a common theme in existentialist philosophy. Nothingness often refers to the fundamental emptiness or lack of meaning that characterizes human existence, while limitedness refers to the finite nature of our existence and the limits placed on our actions, knowledge, and understanding.

In this context, some philosophers argue that our experience of limitedness is intimately connected to our awareness of nothingness. By recognizing the inherent limits of our existence, we come face to face with the emptiness at the core of our being.

However, others argue that our experience of limitedness can actually serve as a source of meaning and significance in the face of nothingness. By accepting our limitations and working within them, we can find purpose and fulfilment in our existence.

Overall, the relationship between nothingness and limitedness is a complex and nuanced philosophical topic that has been explored by many thinkers throughout history. While our experience of limitedness can sometimes serve as a reminder of the emptiness at the core of our being, it can also be a source of meaning and significance as we strive to find purpose and fulfilment within the limits of our existence. Ultimately, it is up to each individual to navigate the complex relationship between nothingness and limitedness in their own lives, and to find a path that leads to a deeper understanding of the human condition.

Nothingness and Liberation

The concept of liberation is closely related to the existentialist idea of nothingness. In existentialist philosophy, nothingness refers to the fundamental emptiness or lack of meaning that characterizes human existence. Liberation, on the other hand, refers to the process of freeing oneself from the constraints and limitations that prevent us from living a fully authentic and meaningful life.

For existentialists, liberation from nothingness requires a recognition of the limits and constraints that shape our existence, as well as a willingness to confront and accept the inherent uncertainty and ambiguity of human life. By embracing the freedom that comes with accepting the reality of our own nothingness, we can begin to create a meaningful existence for ourselves.

However, this process of liberation is often fraught with difficulty and challenge. It requires a willingness to confront our deepest fears and anxieties, as well as a willingness to embrace the unknown and unpredictable nature of human existence.

Ultimately, the goal of liberation is to free ourselves from the constraints of social convention and conformity, and to live our lives in accordance with our deepest values and desires. By embracing our own nothingness, and the freedom that comes with it, we can create a more authentic and meaningful existence for ourselves, and ultimately, find a sense of purpose and fulfilment in life.

Nothingness and Responsibility

The concept of responsibility is closely linked to the idea of nothingness in existentialist philosophy. In this context, nothingness refers to the fundamental emptiness or lack of inherent meaning that characterizes human existence, while responsibility refers to the ability of individuals to make meaningful choices and take actions that shape their own lives.

According to existentialist thinkers, the recognition of our own nothingness creates a sense of responsibility in individuals to take ownership of their own lives and make meaningful choices that reflect their deepest values and desires. Rather than relying on external authorities or societal norms to dictate our actions, existentialists argue that individuals must take responsibility for their own lives and create their own meaning in the face of nothingness.

This process of taking responsibility can be challenging, as it requires individuals to confront their own limitations and the inherent uncertainties of human existence. However, by accepting the reality of our own nothingness, and the responsibility that comes with it, we can begin to create a more authentic and meaningful existence for ourselves.

Ultimately, the goal of taking responsibility in the face of nothingness is to create a sense of purpose and meaning in our lives, and to live in a way that reflects our deepest values and desires. By embracing our own nothingness and taking responsibility for our own existence, we can create a more fulfilling and meaningful life for ourselves and for those around us.

Nothingness and Everything

The relationship between nothingness and everything is a complex philosophical concept that has been explored by many thinkers throughout history. In general, nothingness refers to the fundamental emptiness or lack of inherent meaning that characterizes human existence, while everything refers to the totality of existence, including both material and immaterial aspects of reality.

Some philosophers argue that the concept of nothingness is actually essential to the concept of everything, as the absence of something can only be understood in the context of the existence of everything else. In other words, the recognition of nothingness allows us to appreciate the full richness and complexity of existence.

Others argue that the concept of everything is actually an illusion created by our limited human perception. From this perspective, everything is simply an expression of the underlying nothingness that characterizes the fundamental nature of reality.

Ultimately, the relationship between nothingness and everything is a complex and nuanced philosophical topic that is open to interpretation. Some argue that the concept of nothingness is essential to understanding the full richness and complexity of existence, while others argue that everything is simply an illusion created by our limited human perception. Regardless of one's perspective, it is clear that the relationship between nothingness and everything is an important philosophical concept that has been explored by many thinkers throughout history.

Nothingness and Possibility

In existentialist philosophy, the concept of nothingness is closely linked to the concept of possibility. Nothingness refers to the fundamental emptiness or lack of inherent meaning that characterizes human existence, while possibility refers to the potential for individuals to create meaning and purpose in their lives through their choices and actions.

According to existentialist thinkers, the recognition of nothingness creates a sense of freedom and possibility in individuals to make choices and take actions that shape their own lives. By accepting the fundamental emptiness of existence, individuals are free to create their own meaning and purpose through their choices and actions.

However, this sense of possibility is also accompanied by a sense of responsibility, as individuals must take ownership of their own lives and make meaningful choices that reflect their deepest values and desires.

The relationship between nothingness and possibility is complex and nuanced, and can be interpreted in a variety of ways depending on one's philosophical perspective. Some argue that the recognition of nothingness is essential to the creation of possibility, while others argue that possibility is simply an illusion created by our limited human perception.

Regardless of one's perspective, the relationship between nothingness and possibility is an important philosophical concept that has been explored by many thinkers throughout history. By embracing the freedom and responsibility that comes with the recognition of nothingness, individuals can create a more authentic and meaningful existence for themselves.

Nothingness and Death

The concept of nothingness is often closely associated with death, as death can be seen as the ultimate experience of nothingness. Here are some ways in which nothingness and death can be explored:

1. Nothingness as the cessation of existence: From a materialist perspective, death can be seen as the end of existence, a state in which there is nothing left of the individual. This view of nothingness can be associated with a sense of finality and loss.
2. Nothingness as a gateway to transcendence: From a spiritual or mystical perspective, death can be seen as a gateway to transcendence, a way to move beyond the limitations of the physical world and connect with a deeper level of reality. From this perspective, nothingness can be seen as a potential for spiritual awakening and transformation.
3. Nothingness as a source of fear: For many people, the idea of nothingness can be deeply unsettling, particularly when associated with death. The fear of nothingness can stem from a sense of loss or annihilation, as well as from the uncertainty and unpredictability of death.
4. Nothingness and the impermanence of life: The recognition of the impermanence of all things, including life itself, can be a way to cultivate a deeper appreciation for the present moment and a greater sense of connection to others. From this perspective, nothingness can be seen as a reminder to live fully and embrace the fleeting nature of existence.
5. Nothingness and the mystery of existence: Ultimately, the experience of nothingness can be associated with the mystery of existence, the recognition that there is much we do not understand or cannot explain. From this perspective, nothingness can be seen as an invitation to embrace the unknown and explore the depths of human experience.

Nothingness and God

The concept of nothingness can be approached in different ways in relation to the concept of God, depending on the religious or philosophical perspective. Here are some ways in which nothingness and God can be explored:

1. Nothingness as the absence of God: In some religious or philosophical traditions, nothingness can be seen as the absence of God, a state of spiritual emptiness or separation from the divine. This view of nothingness can be associated with a sense of loss or spiritual longing.

2. Nothingness as a way to approach God: From a mystical or contemplative perspective, nothingness can be seen as a way to approach God, a state of openness and receptivity to the divine. From this perspective, nothingness can be associated with a sense of spiritual freedom and possibility.
3. Nothingness and the transcendent nature of God: Some religious or philosophical traditions emphasize the transcendent nature of God, emphasizing the ways in which God is beyond human comprehension or understanding. From this perspective, nothingness can be seen as a reminder of the limitations of human understanding and the vastness of the divine.
4. Nothingness and the immanent nature of God: Other religious or philosophical traditions emphasize the immanent nature of God, emphasizing the ways in which God is present and active in the world. From this perspective, nothingness can be seen as a way to connect with the divine within ourselves and in the world around us.
5. Nothingness and the mystery of God: Ultimately, the experience of nothingness can be associated with the mystery of God, the recognition that there is much we do not understand or cannot explain about the divine. From this perspective, nothingness can be seen as an invitation to deepen our sense of awe and wonder in the face of the divine mystery.

Nothingness and Evil

The relationship between nothingness and evil is complex and multifaceted. Here are some ways in which nothingness and evil can be explored:

1. Nothingness as a source of evil: Some philosophical and religious traditions see nothingness as a source of evil, or at least as a state that can lead to evil. For example, the absence of love, compassion, or empathy can be seen as a kind of nothingness that can allow for the growth of evil or the perpetration of harm.
2. Nothingness as a consequence of evil: In some religious or philosophical traditions, evil is seen as a force that can separate individuals from the divine, leading to a sense of spiritual emptiness or nothingness. From this perspective, nothingness can be seen as a consequence of evil.
3. Nothingness as a way to confront evil: Some spiritual and philosophical traditions emphasize the importance of confronting the reality of

nothingness as a way to overcome evil. For example, by recognizing the impermanence of all things and cultivating a sense of detachment from worldly desires, individuals can overcome the negative impulses that can lead to harm.

4. Nothingness as a mystery in the face of evil: Ultimately, the experience of nothingness can be associated with the mystery of evil, the recognition that there is much we do not understand or cannot explain about the nature of harm and suffering in the world. From this perspective, nothingness can be seen as an invitation to explore the depths of human experience and confront the challenge of evil with humility and compassion.

Nothingness and Cosmos

The relationship between nothingness and the cosmos is a complex philosophical concept that has been explored by many thinkers throughout history. In general, nothingness refers to the fundamental emptiness or lack of inherent meaning that characterizes human existence, while the cosmos refers to the totality of existence, including both material and immaterial aspects of reality.

Some philosophers argue that the concept of nothingness is actually an essential part of the cosmos, as it provides the necessary contrast and context for the existence of everything else. In other words, without the recognition of nothingness, the full richness and complexity of the cosmos would be impossible to appreciate.

Others argue that the concept of the cosmos is actually an illusion created by our limited human perception. From this perspective, the cosmos is simply an expression of the underlying nothingness that characterizes the fundamental nature of reality.

Ultimately, the relationship between nothingness and the cosmos is a complex and nuanced philosophical topic that is open to interpretation. Some argue that the concept of nothingness is essential to understanding the full richness and complexity of the cosmos, while others argue that the cosmos is simply an illusion created by our limited human perception. Regardless of one's perspective, it is clear that the relationship between nothingness and the cosmos is an important philosophical concept that has been explored by many thinkers throughout history.

Nothingness and Emotions

The relationship between nothingness and emotions is a complex one, as emotions are often seen as a response to the meaning and value that individuals attribute to their experiences, while nothingness refers to the fundamental emptiness or lack of inherent meaning that characterizes human existence.

Some philosophers argue that emotions are actually a way of coping with the recognition of nothingness, as they provide a sense of meaning and purpose in an otherwise empty and meaningless existence. From this perspective, emotions are seen as a way of creating value and significance in a world that is fundamentally devoid of inherent meaning.

Others argue that emotions are actually a hindrance to the recognition of nothingness, as they often cloud our perception and prevent us from seeing reality as it truly is. From this perspective, emotions are seen as a barrier to true understanding and enlightenment, and must be overcome in order to fully embrace the emptiness and nothingness of existence.

Ultimately, the relationship between nothingness and emotions is a complex and nuanced philosophical topic that is open to interpretation. Some argue that emotions are an essential part of coping with the recognition of nothingness, while others argue that they are a hindrance to true understanding and enlightenment. Regardless of one's perspective, it is clear that the relationship between nothingness and emotions is an important philosophical concept that has been explored by many thinkers throughout history.

Nothingness and Energy

The relationship between nothingness and energy is a complex and interesting philosophical concept that has been explored by various thinkers throughout history.

On one hand, energy can be seen as a manifestation of the fundamental emptiness or lack of inherent meaning that characterizes human existence. From this perspective, energy is simply a form of movement and change that arises from the underlying nothingness of reality.

On the other hand, energy can also be seen as a way of creating value and significance in a world that is fundamentally devoid of inherent meaning. From this perspective, energy is seen as a way of transforming and shaping the world around us, giving it a sense of purpose and direction.

Ultimately, the relationship between nothingness and energy is a complex and nuanced philosophical topic that is open to interpretation. Some argue that energy is simply a manifestation of the underlying nothingness of reality, while others argue that it is a way of creating value and significance in an otherwise empty and meaningless existence. Regardless of one's perspective, it is clear that the relationship between nothingness and energy is an important philosophical concept that has been explored by many thinkers throughout history.

Nothingness and Homo sapiens

The concept of nothingness has been explored in relation to the human species, Homo sapiens, in various philosophical and existential contexts. Some thinkers argue that the recognition of nothingness is a fundamental aspect of human existence and consciousness, and that our awareness of the void or emptiness that underlies reality is what sets us apart from other species.

From this perspective, humans are seen as beings who are constantly grappling with the fundamental meaninglessness of existence, and who must create their own meaning and purpose in order to cope with this reality. This recognition of nothingness is seen as a necessary step in the development of human consciousness and self-awareness.

Others argue that the concept of nothingness is simply a human construct, and that it has no inherent meaning or value outside of our own subjective experience. From this perspective, humans are seen as beings who create their own reality through their thoughts and perceptions, rather than simply reflecting or responding to an external reality.

Ultimately, the relationship between nothingness and Homo sapiens is a complex and nuanced philosophical topic that has been explored by many thinkers throughout history. Some argue that the recognition of nothingness is a fundamental aspect of human existence, while others argue that it is simply a subjective construct of the human mind. Regardless of one's perspective, it is clear that the concept of nothingness has played a significant role in shaping our understanding of human consciousness and the nature of reality.

Nothingness and Matter

The relationship between nothingness and matter is a complex and fascinating philosophical topic that has been explored by various thinkers throughout history. On one hand, matter can be seen as a manifestation of the underlying emptiness or void that characterizes reality. From this perspective, matter is simply a form of energy or movement that arises from the underlying nothingness of the universe.

On the other hand, matter can also be seen as a fundamental aspect of reality that has its own inherent properties and characteristics. From this perspective, matter is not simply a manifestation of nothingness, but is rather a distinct and significant aspect of the universe that has its own unique qualities and attributes.

One way of reconciling these two perspectives is to view matter as a dynamic and constantly changing manifestation of the underlying nothingness of the universe. From this perspective, matter is not simply a static and unchanging substance, but is rather a dynamic and evolving process that is constantly in flux.

Ultimately, the relationship between nothingness and matter is a complex and nuanced philosophical topic that is open to interpretation. Some argue that matter is simply a manifestation of the underlying emptiness of the universe, while others argue that it is a distinct and significant aspect of reality that has its own inherent properties and characteristics. Regardless of one's perspective, it is clear that the relationship between nothingness and matter is an important philosophical concept that has been explored by many thinkers throughout history.

Nothingness and Meditation

Meditation is a practice that involves quieting the mind and focusing one's attention in order to achieve a state of mental clarity and relaxation. The concept of nothingness has been closely associated with meditation in many traditions, as practitioners seek to let go of thoughts and distractions in order to achieve a state of emptiness or stillness.

In some forms of meditation, such as Zen and Vipassana, the concept of nothingness is central to the practice. Practitioners are encouraged to focus their attention on their breath or a specific point of concentration, in order to cultivate a state of mindfulness and awareness that transcends the constant chatter of the mind.

The concept of nothingness in meditation is often associated with the idea of letting go of attachments and expectations. By cultivating a state of emptiness or stillness, practitioners are able to let go of their preconceptions and judgments, and simply observe the present moment as it unfolds.

Ultimately, the relationship between nothingness and meditation is a complex and nuanced topic that is open to interpretation. For some practitioners, the concept of nothingness is central to their practice, while for others it may play a more minor role. Regardless of one's perspective, it is clear that meditation can be a powerful tool for cultivating a sense of inner peace and clarity, and that the concept of nothingness can be a useful lens through which to view this practice.

Nothingness and Metaphysics

In metaphysics, nothingness is a concept that has been explored in various ways. Here are some approaches to the relationship between nothingness and metaphysics:

1. Ontological nothingness: Ontology is the branch of metaphysics concerned with the nature of existence. Some philosophers have explored the concept of nothingness in terms of what it means for something to exist or not exist. For example, some argue that nothingness is not a state of existence, but rather a lack of existence.
2. Epistemological nothingness: Epistemology is the branch of metaphysics concerned with knowledge and belief. Some philosophers have explored the concept of nothingness in terms of what can be known or believed about it. For example, some argue that nothingness is beyond our understanding or that we can only know it through negation.
3. Metaphysical nothingness: Metaphysical nothingness refers to the concept of nothingness as it relates to the nature of reality itself. Some philosophers, such as Martin Heidegger, have argued that nothingness is an essential part of human existence and consciousness, and that it is an inherent part of the structure of reality.
4. Nothingness and the nature of being: Some philosophers have explored the relationship between nothingness and the nature of being. For example, some argue that nothingness is necessary for the existence of being, as without nothingness, being would be unable to distinguish itself from other forms of existence. Others have explored the idea that nothingness is a fundamental aspect of being itself, and that being and nothingness are two sides of the same coin.

Nothingness and Nature

Nothingness and nature are two concepts that can be explored in various contexts, including philosophy, spirituality, and science. Here are some ways to approach each concept:

Nothingness:

1. Philosophical nothingness: In philosophy, nothingness refers to the absence or negation of something, such as the absence of existence or

the absence of meaning. Some philosophers, such as Martin Heidegger, have argued that nothingness is an essential part of human existence and consciousness.
2. Scientific nothingness: In science, nothingness can refer to a vacuum or a space devoid of matter or energy. The concept of nothingness has also been explored in physics, particularly in theories about the origin of the universe and the nature of reality.
3. Spiritual nothingness: In spiritual traditions, nothingness can refer to a state of emptiness or nonattachment. For example, in Buddhism, the concept of "emptiness" refers to the idea that all things are empty of inherent existence and that clinging to the idea of self or identity leads to suffering.

Nature:

1. Physical nature: Nature refers to the physical world and all its phenomena, including living organisms, landscapes, and natural resources. It encompasses everything from the smallest particles to the largest ecosystems.
2. Human nature: Human nature refers to the innate characteristics and tendencies that define human beings, such as the capacity for language, socialization, and morality.
3. Spiritual nature: In spiritual traditions, nature can have a deeper, symbolic meaning. For example, nature can be seen as a manifestation of the divine or as a symbol of the interconnectedness of all things. In some traditions, connecting with nature is seen as a path to spiritual growth and enlightenment.

Nothingness and ologies

The concept of nothingness can be explored in various fields of study, including several ologies. Here are some ways that the concept of nothingness can relate to different ologies:

1. Cosmology: In cosmology, the concept of nothingness can relate to the origins of the universe. Some cosmologists argue that the universe began from a state of nothingness or that there was a state of nothingness before the Big Bang.

2. Epistemology: Epistemology is the study of knowledge and belief. In epistemology, the concept of nothingness can relate to questions about what can be known or believed about nothingness itself, and whether it is possible to have knowledge or beliefs about it.
3. Psychology: In psychology, the concept of nothingness can relate to questions about the nature of consciousness and the self. Some psychologists argue that the experience of nothingness, or a sense of emptiness, is a common aspect of human existence and may be related to feelings of anxiety or depression.

Nothingness and Ontology

In ontology, the concept of nothingness can be explored in various ways. Here are some approaches to the relationship between nothingness and ontology:

1. Nothingness as non-existence: Some ontologists argue that nothingness is simply the absence of existence. From this perspective, nothingness is not a positive entity, but rather the negation of being.
2. Nothingness as potentiality: Other ontologists argue that nothingness is a necessary aspect of being. From this perspective, nothingness can be seen as a kind of potentiality, a space of openness or possibility that allows for the emergence of being.
3. Nothingness and the nature of being: Some ontologists argue that nothingness is essential to the nature of being itself. From this perspective, being and nothingness are two sides of the same coin, and it is impossible to understand the nature of being without also understanding the nature of nothingness.
4. Nothingness and the limits of knowledge: Some ontologists argue that nothingness is beyond our capacity to understand or know. From this perspective, nothingness is not simply the absence of something, but rather a kind of limit or boundary that marks the limits of human knowledge and understanding.
5. Nothingness and the possibility of non-being: Some ontologists argue that nothingness is a kind of alternative or potential state of being, a possibility that is always present alongside actual existence. From this perspective, nothingness is not simply the negation of being, but rather a kind of alternative mode of existence that is always present alongside actual existence.

Nothingness and Reality

The concept of nothingness can be explored in various ways in relation to reality. Here are some approaches to the relationship between nothingness and reality:

1. Nothingness as absence: One approach to nothingness and reality is to view nothingness as the absence of something. From this perspective, nothingness is not a positive entity, but rather a lack or negation of something that is real.
2. Nothingness as a fundamental aspect of reality: Another approach is to view nothingness as a fundamental aspect of reality itself. Some philosophers argue that nothingness is an inherent part of the structure of reality, and that without nothingness, reality could not exist as we know it.
3. Nothingness and the limits of reality: Some philosophers argue that nothingness is a kind of limit or boundary that defines the limits of reality. From this perspective, nothingness is not simply the absence of something, but rather a kind of boundary or limit that marks the edge of what is real or knowable.
4. Nothingness and the possibility of alternative realities: Some philosophers argue that nothingness is a kind of alternative reality, a space of openness or possibility that allows for the emergence of new forms of reality. From this perspective, nothingness is not simply the absence of something, but rather a kind of potentiality that allows for the emergence of new realities.
5. Nothingness and the nature of perception: Some philosophers argue that nothingness is not simply the absence of something, but rather a kind of positive experience or perception. From this perspective, nothingness is not simply the absence of objects, but rather a kind of perceptual experience in which the absence of objects is itself an object of perception.

Nothingness and Sciences

The concept of nothingness can be explored in various ways in relation to different fields of science. Here are some approaches to the relationship between nothingness and sciences:

1. Physics: In physics, the concept of nothingness can relate to questions about the nature of the universe and the origins of the universe. Some physicists argue that the universe began from a state of nothingness, or that there was a state of nothingness before the Big Bang. Other physicists explore the nature of empty space, which can be thought of as a kind of nothingness.
2. Biology: In biology, the concept of nothingness can relate to questions about the origins of life and the nature of consciousness. Some biologists explore the possibility that life emerged from a state of nothingness, or that consciousness is a kind of "nothingness" that emerges from the complexity of the brain.
3. Computer Science: In computer science, the concept of nothingness can relate to questions about the nature of computation and the limits of artificial intelligence. Some computer scientists explore the possibility of creating algorithms that can generate something from nothing, while others argue that there are limits to what can be achieved through computation.
4. Philosophy of Science: In the philosophy of science, the concept of nothingness can relate to questions about the nature of scientific inquiry and the limits of scientific knowledge. Some philosophers of science argue that the concept of nothingness is essential to scientific inquiry, while others see it as a kind of limit or boundary that marks the limits of scientific understanding.

Nothingness and Sexuality

The concept of nothingness can be explored in various ways in relation to sexuality. Here are some approaches to the relationship between nothingness and sexuality:

1. Nothingness as a lack: In some philosophical and psychoanalytic approaches, sexuality can be seen as a desire for something that is lacking or absent, and this lack or absence can be thought of as a kind of nothingness. From this perspective, sexuality is driven by a desire to fill this nothingness with pleasure or satisfaction.
2. Nothingness and vulnerability: In some feminist and queer theories, sexuality can be seen as a way to embrace vulnerability and the experience of nothingness. From this perspective, sexuality can be a way to explore the limits of the self and embrace the possibility of being

transformed or undone by the experience of intimacy with others.

3. Nothingness and pleasure: In some erotic and sensual practices, sexuality can be seen as a way to embrace the nothingness of the present moment and experience pleasure in the absence of thought or self-awareness. This can be thought of as a kind of mindfulness practice that allows for a deeper connection to the body and the present moment.
4. Nothingness and taboo: In some cultural contexts, sexuality can be associated with nothingness or emptiness through taboos or prohibitions. From this perspective, the experience of sexuality is seen as something that threatens the order of society and can be associated with a kind of emptiness or loss of control.

Nothingness and Soul

The concept of nothingness can be explored in various ways in relation to the idea of the soul. Here are some approaches to the relationship between nothingness and the soul:

1. Nothingness as a void within the soul: In some spiritual or philosophical traditions, the soul can be seen as a container for the self or consciousness, and this container can be thought of as having an inner void or nothingness. From this perspective, the experience of emptiness or nothingness within the soul can be a way to access deeper levels of consciousness or spirituality.
2. Nothingness and the dissolution of the soul: In some mystical or spiritual traditions, the experience of nothingness can be associated with the dissolution of the self or the soul. From this perspective, the soul is seen as a kind of construct or illusion that must be dissolved in order to access a deeper level of spiritual truth.
3. Nothingness and the immortality of the soul: In some religious or philosophical traditions, the soul is seen as immortal and eternal, and the experience of nothingness can be a way to access this eternal aspect of the soul. From this perspective, nothingness can be thought of as a kind of doorway to a deeper level of existence beyond the material world.
4. Nothingness and the shadow self: In some psychological or spiritual approaches, the experience of nothingness can be associated with the shadow self or the darker aspects of the soul. From this perspective, exploring the experience of nothingness within the soul can be a way to confront and integrate these shadow aspects of the self.

5. Nothingness and the unity of the soul: In some spiritual or philosophical traditions, the experience of nothingness can be associated with the unity of the soul with the divine or the universe. From this perspective, the experience of nothingness can be a way to transcend the individual self and access a deeper level of interconnectedness with all of existence.

Nothingness and Spirit

The concept of nothingness can be explored in various ways in relation to the idea of spirit. Here are some approaches to the relationship between nothingness and spirit:

1. Nothingness as the essence of spirit: In some spiritual or philosophical traditions, nothingness can be seen as the essential nature of spirit. From this perspective, spirit is not a concrete entity but rather a formless and transcendent essence that exists beyond the material world.
2. Nothingness as the ground of spirit: In some spiritual or philosophical traditions, nothingness can be seen as the ground of all being, including spirit. From this perspective, spirit arises from the underlying emptiness or void of the universe and is a manifestation of the cosmic creative energy.
3. Nothingness and the dissolution of spirit: In some mystical or spiritual traditions, the experience of nothingness can be associated with the dissolution of the self or spirit. From this perspective, the ego or the sense of individual identity must be dissolved in order to access a deeper level of spiritual truth.
4. Nothingness and the unity of spirit: In some spiritual or philosophical traditions, the experience of nothingness can be associated with the unity of spirit with the divine or the universe. From this perspective, the experience of nothingness can be a way to transcend the individual self and access a deeper level of interconnectedness with all of existence.

Nothingness and Spirituality

The concept of nothingness can be explored in various ways in relation to spirituality. Here are some approaches to the relationship between nothingness and spirituality:

1. Nothingness as a pathway to spiritual experience: In some spiritual traditions, the experience of nothingness can be a pathway to deeper

spiritual experiences. Through practices such as meditation or contemplation, individuals may be able to access a state of emptiness or nothingness that can allow them to connect with the divine or access a deeper level of spiritual truth.

2. Nothingness as a way to transcend the ego: In some spiritual or philosophical traditions, the experience of nothingness can be associated with the dissolution of the ego or the sense of individual identity. From this perspective, the ego must be dissolved in order to access a deeper level of spiritual truth and unity with the divine or the universe.
3. Nothingness and the impermanence of all things: In some spiritual or philosophical traditions, the experience of nothingness can be associated with the impermanence of all things. From this perspective, the experience of emptiness or nothingness can be a way to confront the transitory nature of existence and cultivate a deeper sense of acceptance and peace.
4. Nothingness and the interconnectedness of all things: In some spiritual or philosophical traditions, the experience of nothingness can be associated with the interconnectedness of all things. From this perspective, the experience of emptiness or nothingness can be a way to recognize the essential unity of all existence and cultivate a sense of compassion and empathy for all beings.
5. Nothingness and the mystery of existence: In some spiritual or philosophical traditions, the experience of nothingness can be associated with the mystery of existence. From this perspective, the experience of emptiness or nothingness can be a way to embrace the inherent uncertainty and unpredictability of life and connect with a deeper sense of wonder and awe for the universe.

Nothingness and Substance

The concept of nothingness can be explored in various ways in relation to substance. Here are some approaches to the relationship between nothingness and substance:

1. Nothingness as the absence of substance: In some philosophical traditions, nothingness can be seen as the absence of substance. From this perspective, substance is defined as anything that exists or has being, while nothingness is the absence of being or existence.

2. Nothingness and the limits of substance: In some philosophical traditions, the experience of nothingness can be associated with the limits of substance. From this perspective, substance is seen as limited and finite, while nothingness is infinite and boundless. The experience of nothingness can thus be a way to confront the limitations of substance and recognize the possibility of something beyond the material world.
3. Nothingness and the illusion of substance: In some philosophical traditions, the experience of nothingness can be associated with the illusion of substance. From this perspective, substance is seen as a temporary and illusory construct, while nothingness is the ultimate reality. The experience of nothingness can thus be a way to strip away the illusions of substance and connect with a deeper level of reality.
4. Nothingness and the paradox of substance: In some philosophical traditions, the experience of nothingness can be associated with the paradox of substance. From this perspective, substance is both necessary for existence and yet ultimately insufficient to explain the nature of reality. The experience of nothingness can thus be a way to confront the paradox of substance and embrace the mystery of existence.
5. Nothingness and the potential for substance: In some philosophical traditions, the experience of nothingness can be associated with the potential for substance. From this perspective, nothingness is not an absence or lack but rather a potentiality that can give rise to substance. The experience of nothingness can thus be a way to connect with the creative potential of the universe and recognize the possibility of something emerging from nothing.

Nothingness and Yoga

In yoga philosophy, the concept of nothingness can be explored in various ways. Here are some approaches to the relationship between nothingness and yoga:

1. Nothingness as the goal of yoga: In some branches of yoga, such as Jnana Yoga, the ultimate goal is to attain a state of nothingness or emptiness, known as "nirvana" or "Samadhi." This state is characterized by a complete dissolution of the ego and a merging with the divine or the universe.
2. Nothingness as the starting point of yoga: In some branches of yoga, such as Hatha Yoga, the practice begins with the recognition of the

fundamental emptiness or nothingness of existence. From this starting point, the practice is designed to cultivate greater awareness, vitality, and connection to the universe.

3. Nothingness as a way to transcend the limitations of the body and mind: In some branches of yoga, such as Kundalini Yoga, the practice is designed to activate the energy centers of the body and move beyond the limitations of the physical and mental realms. From this perspective, the experience of nothingness can be a way to transcend the limitations of the body and mind and access a deeper level of spiritual truth.
4. Nothingness and the unity of all things: In some branches of yoga, such as Bhakti Yoga, the experience of nothingness can be associated with the recognition of the essential unity of all things. From this perspective, the experience of emptiness or nothingness can be a way to cultivate a deeper sense of compassion and connection to all beings.
5. Nothingness and the impermanence of all things: In some branches of yoga, such as Vinyasa Yoga, the practice is designed to flow with the impermanence of existence and cultivate a deep acceptance of change. From this perspective, the experience of nothingness can be a way to embrace the inherent uncertainty and unpredictability of life and find a sense of peace in the midst of it all.

FOUR
NOTHINGNESS AND MAJOR RELIGIONS

Nothingness and Buddhism

In Buddhism, the concept of nothingness is closely related to the doctrine of "emptiness" or "voidness" (shunyata). Emptiness refers to the idea that all phenomena lack inherent existence or self-nature, and are instead dependent on other causes and conditions.

According to Buddhist teachings, the realization of emptiness can lead to liberation from suffering and the cycle of birth and death. By recognizing the emptiness of all phenomena, one can overcome attachment, aversion, and ignorance, and attain a state of inner peace and wisdom.

The concept of nothingness is also related to the Buddhist practice of meditation, which involves cultivating a state of mental clarity and stillness. In meditation, one can observe the arising and passing away of thoughts and sensations, and recognize the impermanence and emptiness of all phenomena.

Overall, the concept of nothingness in Buddhism can be seen as a means of transcending the limitations of the ego and realizing the interconnectedness of all things. It is a fundamental aspect of Buddhist philosophy and practice, and has inspired many practitioners to seek a deeper understanding of the nature of reality and the path to liberation.

Nothingness and Christianity

In Christianity, the concept of nothingness can be seen as related to the idea of humility and self-emptying, which is a central theme in the teachings of Jesus Christ. The concept of nothingness can be understood as the idea of surrendering one's own desires and ego to the will of God, and embracing a state of openness and receptivity to divine grace.

The concept of nothingness can be seen in various ways, depending on the theological tradition and context. One interpretation of nothingness in Christian thought is related to the concept of "kenosis," which is the self-emptying of Christ as described in the New Testament. According to this view, Christ emptied himself of his divine attributes in order to become human and sacrifice himself for humanity's salvation. This act of self-emptying is seen as an expression of divine love and humility.

For example, in the Gospel of Matthew, Jesus says, "Blessed are the poor in spirit, for theirs is the kingdom of heaven" (Matthew 5:3). This verse can be interpreted as a call to embrace a state of spiritual poverty or nothingness, in which one recognizes one's own limitations and emptiness, and relies on God's mercy and grace for salvation.

In some Christian mystical traditions, the concept of nothingness is related to the idea of "divine union," where the individual seeks to transcend the ego and merge with God in a state of pure being. This state of nothingness is seen as a way of experiencing the divine presence and achieving spiritual transformation.

Another interpretation of nothingness in Christian thought is related to the idea of "nothingness before God." According to this view, human beings are created out of nothing by God's will, and our existence is dependent on God's grace. In this sense, the concept of nothingness can be seen as a recognition of our dependence on God and a call to surrender our will to God's.

The concept of nothingness is also related to the Christian contemplative tradition, which involves the practice of prayer, meditation, and silence. In contemplative prayer, one seeks to let go of one's own thoughts and desires, and to open oneself to God's presence and guidance.

Overall, the concept of nothingness in Christianity can be seen as a means of cultivating a deeper relationship with God, and of recognizing one's own dependence on divine grace. It is a fundamental aspect of Christian spirituality, and has inspired many believers to seek a deeper understanding of the mystery of God's love and presence in their lives.

Nothingness and Hebrew

In Hebrew thought, the concept of nothingness is related to the idea of "ayin," which means "nothingness" or "emptiness." Ayin is also used to refer to the infinite and indescribable nature of God, which transcends human comprehension.

In Hebrew thought and language, the concept of nothingness is expressed through the term "tohu va'vohu," which appears in the opening verses of the Book of Genesis. This phrase is often translated as "formless and void," and describes the state of the universe before God created light and separated the waters from the land.

In the Jewish mystical tradition of Kabbalah, the concept of ayin is related to the idea of "Ein Sof," which means "infinite" or "limitless." Ein Sof is seen as the ultimate reality of God's existence, which is beyond all finite forms and categories.

The concept of nothingness is also related to the Jewish practice of meditation and contemplation, which involves emptying the mind of all distractions and focusing on the divine presence. This state of nothingness is seen as a way of experiencing the transcendence of God's existence and achieving spiritual transformation.

Overall, the concept of nothingness in Hebrew thought can be seen as a way of recognizing the limitations of human knowledge and understanding, and surrendering to the mystery of God's presence. It is a fundamental aspect of Jewish theology and practice, and has inspired many practitioners to seek a deeper understanding of the nature of God and the path to spiritual enlightenment.

Nothingness and Hinduism

In Hinduism, the concept of nothingness is closely related to the idea of "Brahman," which is the ultimate reality and source of all existence. Brahman is often described as an absolute nothingness or emptiness, which contains the potential for all creation.

The concept of nothingness is also related to the Hindu practice of meditation, which involves the cultivation of a state of inner stillness and awareness. Through meditation, the individual seeks to quiet the mind and overcome the distractions and illusions of the ego. This state of nothingness is seen as a way of experiencing the divine presence and achieving spiritual transformation.

In Hindu philosophical traditions, Advaita Vedanta, which is a non-dualistic school of Hindu philosophy, the concept of nothingness is related to the idea of "neti neti," which means "not this, not that." According to this view, ultimate reality cannot be described or understood through language or concepts, and can only be realized through direct experience.

Overall, the concept of nothingness in Hinduism can be seen as a way of recognizing the ultimate reality of Brahman and the limitations of human understanding. It is a fundamental aspect of Hindu theology and practice, and has inspired many practitioners to seek a deeper understanding of the nature of reality and the path to spiritual transformation.

Nothingness and Islam

In Islam, the concept of nothingness is related to the idea of *tawhid*, which is the belief in the oneness and unity of God. *Tawhid* is a fundamental tenet of Islamic theology, and is seen as a way of transcending the limitations of the ego and recognizing the ultimate reality of God's existence.

The concept of nothingness is also related to the Islamic practice of *zikr*, or remembrance of God. Through the repetition of God's name and the contemplation of God's attributes, the individual seeks to cultivate a state of mindfulness and awareness of God's presence. This state of nothingness is seen as a way of purifying the heart and achieving spiritual transformation.

In Sufism, which is the mystical tradition of Islam, the concept of nothingness is related to the idea of *fana*, which is the annihilation of the ego in the presence of God. *Fana* is seen as a way of achieving union with God and experiencing the divine presence.

Overall, the concept of nothingness in Islam can be seen as a way of transcending the limitations of the ego and recognizing the ultimate reality of God's existence. It is a fundamental aspect of Islamic theology and practice, and has inspired many practitioners to seek a deeper understanding of the nature of God and the path to spiritual transformation.

Bibliography

Alt, K. W., & Rossbach, A. (2009). Nothing in nature is as consistent as change. In *Comparative Dental Morphology* (Vol. 13, pp. 190-196). Karger Publishers.

Altizer, T. J. (1966). *The gospel of Christian atheism* (pp. 216-18). Philadelphia: Westminster Press.

Armstrong, J. K. (2016). *Seinfeldia: how a show about nothing changed everything*. Simon and Schuster.

Arnold, D. (2005). The Cult of Nothingness: The Philosophers and the Buddha.

Baillie, J. (2020). The recognition of nothingness. *Philosophical Studies, 177*(9), 2585-2603.

Baudrillard, J. (1983). The precession of simulacra. *New York*.

Baudrillard, J., Foss, P., Patton, P., & Beitchman, P. (1983). *Simulations* (p. 1). New York: Semiotext (e).

Beck, M. (1946). Existentialism, rationalism, and Christian faith. *The Journal of Religion, 26*(4), 283-295.

Beebee, H. (2004). Causing and nothingness.

Bellusci, D. (2014). Transcendence and Nothingness. *Études maritainiennes/Maritain Studies, 30*, 40-52.

Berdyaev, N. (1957). Unground and Freedom. *CrossCurrents, 7*(3), 247-262.

Bilimoria, P. (2010). Hegel's Spectre on Indian Thought and its God-in-Nothingness. *Religions of South Asia, 4*(2), 199-211.

Bjarnason, P. E. (2003). Epicurus' second remedy:" Death is nothing to us". *Akroterion, 48*(1), 21-44.

Butler, J. (1985). Variations on sex and gender: Behaviour Wittig, and Foucault. *Praxis International, 5*(4), 505-516.

Cagri, T. M. (2012). Existentialism in two plays of Jean-Paul Sartre. *International Journal of English and Literature, 3*(3), 50-54.

Campbell, S. M. (2012). *The Early Heidegger's Philosophy of Life: Facticity, Being, and Language: Facticity, Being, and Language*. Fordham Univ Press.

Caputo, J. D. (1975). The Nothingness of the Intellect in Meister Eckhart's" Parisian Questions". *The Thomist: A Speculative Quarterly Review, 39*(1), 85-115.

Carroll, W. E. (1988). Big bang cosmology, quantum tunneling from nothing, and creation. *Laval théologique et philosophique, 44*(1), 59-75.

Carter, R. E. (2009). God and nothingness. *Philosophy East and West*, 1-21.

Casati, F., & Priest, G. (2018). Heidegger and Dōgen on the Ineffable. In *The Significance of Indeterminacy* (pp. 279-308). Routledge.

Catalano, J. S. (1985). *A commentary on Jean-Paul Sartre's Being and nothingness*. University of Chicago Press.

Cerbone, D. R. (2014). *Understanding phenomenology*. Routledge.

Chai, D. (2019). Nothingness and Selfhood in the Zhuangzi. *The Bloomsbury research handbook of early Chinese ethics and political philosophy*, 133-154.

Chai, D. (2019). *Zhuangzi and the Becoming of Nothingness*. Suny Press.

Chan, W. T. (2015). *The Way of Lao Tzu*. Ravenio Books.

Childs, P. (2016). *Modernism*. Routledge.

Chittick, W. C. (2005). *The sufi doctrine of Rumi*. World Wisdom, Inc.

Chittick, W. C. (2010). *The Sufi path of knowledge: Ibn al-Arabi's metaphysics of imagination*. State University of New York Press.

Chittick, W. C. (2012). *Ibn'Arabi: Heir to the prophets*. Simon and Schuster.

Churchill, S., & Reynolds, J. (2014). *Jean-Paul Sartre: Key Concepts*. Routledge.

Clark, T. W. (1994). Death, nothingness, and subjectivity. *The Humanist*, 54(6), 15-20.

Coleridge, S. T. (1984). *Biographia literaria, or, Biographical sketches of my literary life and opinions* (Vol. 7). Princeton University Press.

Correia, F., & Rosenkranz, S. (2018). *Nothing to Come*. Berlin: Springer.

Corrington, R. S. (2017). *Nature and nothingness: An essay in ordinal phenomenology*. Lexington Books.

Critchley, S. (2004). *Very little... almost nothing: death, philosophy and literature*. Routledge.

Dallmayr, F. (1992). Nothingness and śūnyatā: a comparison of Heidegger and Nishitani. *Philosophy East and West*, 37-48.

Deleuze, G. (2006). *Nietzsche and philosophy*. Columbia University Press.

Deleuze, G., & Guattari, F. (2000). From What is Philosophy?. *Continental Philosophy of Science*, 258.

Derrida, J. (1969). The ends of man. *Philosophy and phenomenological research*, *30*(1), 31-57.

Derrida, J. (1983). Geschlecht sexual difference, ontological difference. *Research in Phenomenology*, *13*(1), 65-83.

Descartes, R. (1984). *The Philosophical Writings of Descartes: Volume 2* (Vol. 2). Cambridge University Press.

Drucker, P. F. (1949). The unfashionable Kierkegaard. *The Sewanee Review*, *57*(4), 587-602.

Duclow, D. F. (1977). Divine nothingness and self-creation in John Scotus Eriugena. *The Journal of Religion*, *57*(2), 109-123.

Dussel, E. (2003). *Philosophy of liberation*. Wipf and Stock Publishers.

Eagleton, T. (1986). Capitalism, modernism and postmodernism. *Jean-François Lyotard: Critical Evaluations in Cultural Theory. Vol. 2, Politics and History of Philosophy*, 127-141.

Eagleton, T. (1990). *The ideology of the aesthetic* (Vol. 23). Blackwell: Oxford.

Edwards, P., Freeman, E., & Sugden, S. J. (1979). *Heidegger on death: a critical evaluation*. La Salle: Hegeler Institute.

Einstein, A., von Neumann, J., Bohr, N., Tesla, N., Gödel, K., Planck, M., & Bacon, F. Could Be "Nothing" the Origin of "Everything"?.

Erhard, C. (2020). Negation, nonbeing, and nothingness 1. In *The Sartrean Mind* (pp. 172-185). Routledge.

Froman, W. J. (1981). Heidegger and Sartre: An Essay on Being and Place. By Joseph P. Fell. *The Modern Schoolman*, *58*(4), 271-276.

Gardner, S. (1991). The unconscious. *The Cambridge Companion to Freud*, 136-60.

Gardner, S. (2009). *Sartre's' being and nothingness': A reader's guide.* Bloomsbury Publishing.

Giles, M. T. (2020). *The Politics of the Fall in St. Augustine of Hippo.* Michigan State University.

Giorgi, A., & Giorgi, B. (2003). *Phenomenology*. Sage Publications, Inc.

Grego, R. F. (1997). *Jiddu Krishnamurti and Thich Nhat Hanh on the silence of God and the human condition*. State University of New York at Albany.

Hanh, T. N. (2008). *Transformation and Healing: Sutra on the Four Establishments of Mindfulness: Easy read Super Large 24pt Edition*. Read How You Want. com.

Heisig, J. W. (2001). *Philosophers of nothingness: An essay on the Kyoto School*. University of Hawaii Press.

Henry, D. P. (1965). Saint Anselm and nothingness. *The Philosophical Quarterly (1950-)*, *15*(60), 243-246.

Holst, M. A. (2021). "To be is to inter-be": Thich Nhat Hanh on interdependent arising. *Journal of World Philosophies*, *6*(2), 17-30.

Howells, C. (2010). *Sartre and Death: Forgetting the Mortal Body in Being and Nothingness* (pp. 130-138). Palgrave Macmillan UK.

Hoy, R. C. (2001). Parmenides' complete rejection of Time. *The Importance of Time: Proceedings of the Philosophy of Time Society, 1995–2000*, 105-129.

James, W. (1904). Does' consciousness' exist?. *The Journal of philosophy, psychology and scientific methods, 1*(18), 477-491.

Kantorowicz, H. (1934). Some rationalism about realism. *The Yale Law Journal, 43*(8), 1240-1253.

Kanu, I. A. (2012). The problem of being in metaphysics. *African Research Review, 6*(2), 113-122.

Kasulis, T. P., Yasuo, Y., & Yuasa, Y. (1987). *The body: Toward an Eastern mind-body theory*. Suny Press.

Kaya, Ç. (2016). Rumi from the viewpoint of spiritual psychology and counseling. *Spiritual Psychology and Counseling, 1*(1), 9-25.

Kean, C. (2009). Silencing the self: schizophrenia as a self-disturbance. *Schizophrenia bulletin, 35*(6), 1034-1036.

Kenny, A. (1985). *The philosophical writings of Descartes* (Vol. 1, pp. 1984-1985). Cambridge: Cambridge University Press.

Khrennikov, A. (1998). Human subconscious as ap-adic dynamical system. *Journal of Theoretical Biology, 193*(2), 179-196.

Kim, S. C. (1974). *Notion of Nothingness in M. Heidegger and Lao-Tzu* (Doctoral dissertation, Oklahoma State University).

Kopf, G. (2002). Temporality and Personal Identity in the Thought of Nishida Kitarō. *Philosophy East and West*, 224-245.

Kopf, G. (2014). Zen, philosophy, and emptiness: Dōgen and the deconstruction of concepts. In *Nothingness in Asian philosophy* (pp. 246-262). Routledge.

Kovács, A. B. (2006). Sartre, the philosophy of nothingness, and the modern melodrama. *The Journal of aesthetics and art criticism, 64*(1), 135-145.

Kraft, W. F. (1974). A psychology of nothingness.philpapers.org

Krishnamurti, J., & Bohm, D. (1999). *The limits of thought: discussions*. Psychology Press.

Krishnamurti, J., & Bohm, D. (2002). Living in truth. In *The Limits of Thought* (pp. 3-27). Routledge.

Kuhn, H. (2019). *Encounter with nothingness: an essay on existentialism*. Routledge.

Kuhn, H. (2019). *Encounter with nothingness: an essay on existentialism*. Routledge.

Lacoue-Labarthe, P., & Nancy, J. L. (1988). *The literary absolute: the theory of literature in German romanticism*. suny Press.

Lama, D. (2005). *The universe in a single atom: The convergence of science and spirituality*. Harmony.

Lama, D. (2009). *The middle way: Faith grounded in reason*. Simon and Schuster.

Lanzetta, B. J. (1992). Three categories of nothingness in Eckhart. *The Journal of Religion*, *72*(2), 248-268.

Lau, K. Y. (2020). Nothingness. In *The Routledge Handbook of Phenomenology and Phenomenological Philosophy* (pp. 316-323). Routledge.

Laycock, S. W. (2012). *Nothingness and emptiness: A Buddhist engagement with the ontology of Jean-Paul Sartre*. State University of New York Press.

Leibniz, G. W. (2010). *Theodicy*. Cosimo, Inc..

Leibniz, G. W. (2015). *Leibniz: Philosophical Essays*. Hackett publishing.

Leibniz, G. W., & Leibniz, G. W. (1989). *Discourse on Metaphysics: 1686* (pp. 303-330). Springer Netherlands.

Leung, K. H. (2020). Transcendentality and Nothingness in Sartre's Atheistic Ontology. *Philosophy*, *95*(4), 471-495.

Levin, P. A., & Taheri-Araghi, S. (2019). One is nothing without the other: theoretical and empirical analysis of cell growth and cell cycle progression. *Journal of molecular biology*, *431*(11), 2061-2067.

Levinas, E. (1979). *Totality and infinity: An essay on exteriority* (Vol. 1). Springer Science & Business Media.

Levinas, E. (1987). Transcendence and evil. In *Collected philosophical papers* (pp. 175-186). Dordrecht: Springer Netherlands.

Liu, R. (2022). Three interpretations of freedom in Sartre's Being and Nothingness. *The Humanistic Psychologist*, *50*(2), 179.

Locke, E. A. (1975). Personnel attitudes and motivation. *Annual review of psychology*, *26*(1), 457-480.

Lombardi, R. (2010). The body emerging from the "neverland" of nothingness. *The Psychoanalytic Quarterly*, *79*(4), 879-909.

Long, E. T. (1999). Quest for transcendence. *International journal for philosophy of religion*, 51-65.

Loy, D. (1982). Enlightenment in Buddhism and Advaita Vedanta: Are Nirvana and Moksha the Same?. *International Philosophical Quarterly*, *22*(1), 65-74.

Lyotard, J. F. (1985). The sublime and the avant garde. *Paragraph*, *6*(1), 1-18.

Lyotard, J. F. (1988). *Le différend* (Vol. 46). U of Minnesota Press.

Lyotard, J. F. (2000). Can Thought go on without a Body?. In *Posthumanism* (pp. 129-140). Palgrave, London.

Madan, D. (2016). The Absurdity of the Absurd: The Meta Narrative of Nothingness. *International Journal and Studies in English Language and Literature*, *4*(3), 18-21.

Maftei, S. (2013). “Nothingness or a God”: Nihilism, Enlightenment, and “Natural Reason” in Friedrich Heinrich Jacobi’s Works. *Meta: research in hermeneutics, phenomenology, and practical philosophy vol*, (2), 279-297.

Marsh, W. E. (2009). *Nothingness, metanarrative, and possibility*. Author House.

Matuštík, M. B., Matuštík, M. J., & Westphal, M. (Eds.). (1995). *Kierkegaard in post/modernity*. Indiana University Press.

McDaniel, K. (2010). Being and almost nothingness. *Noûs*, *44*(4), 628-649.

Merleau-Ponty, M. (1964). *Sense and non-sense*. Northwestern University Press.

Merleau-Ponty, M. (1968). *The visible and the invisible: Followed by working notes*. Northwestern University Press.

Mills, K. L. (2009). 'Between pain and nothing, I choose nothing: Trauma, post-traumatic stress disorder and substance use.

Morgan, M. (2017). Leo Stan, Either Nothingness or Love: On Alterity in Søren Kierkegaard’s Writings. In *Volume 18, Tome III: Kierkegaard Secondary Literature* (pp. 219-224). Routledge.

Moten, F. (2013). Blackness and nothingness (mysticism in the flesh). *South Atlantic Quarterly*, *112*(4), 737-780.

Nancy, J. L. (1993). *The experience of freedom*. Stanford University Press.

Nelson, E. S. (2023). Martin Heidegger and Kitayama Junyū: Nothingness, Emptiness, and the Thing. *Asian Studies*, *11*(1), 27-50.

Nietzsche, F. W. (2005). *The Anti-Christ*. Cosimo, Inc..

Nishida, K. (1973). *Intelligibility and the Philosophy of Nothingness.*

Nishitani, K. (1982). *Religion and nothingness*. Univ of California Press.

Nivison, D. S. (1973). Moral decision in Wang Yang-Ming: The problem of chinese" existentialism". *Philosophy East and West*, *23*(1/2), 121-137.

Norman, J. (2002). Nietzsche and early romanticism. *Journal of the History of Ideas*, *63*(3), 501-519.

Notomi, N. (2007). *Plato on what is not* (pp. 254-75). Festschrift for Myles Burnyeat], Oxford: Oxford University Press.

Novak, M. (1970). *The experience of nothingness*. Transaction Publishers.

Olivier, A. (2018). The Freedom of Facticity. *Religions*, *9*(4), 110.

Pattison, G., & Kirkpatrick, K. (2018). *The Mystical Sources of Existentialist Thought: Being, Nothingness, Love*. Routledge.

Phillips, E. D. (1955). Parmenides on thought and being. *The Philosophical Review, 64*(4), 546-560.

Pricopi, V. A. (2018). Augustine of Hippo on creatio ex nihilo. *Agathos, 9*(1), 35-44.

Quindlen, A. (2002). Doing nothing is something. *Newsweek, 139*(19), 76-76.

Rankine, C. (1994). *Nothing in nature is private* (Vol. 44). Cleveland St U Poetry Cntr.

Reginster, B. (2021). *The Will to Nothingness: An Essay on Nietzsche's On the Genealogy of Morality*. Oxford University Press.

Ricoeur, P. (1996). In Memoriam Emmanuel Levinas. *Philosophy Today, 40*(3), 331-333.

Rigsby, C. A. (2014). Three Strands of Nothingness in Chinese Philosophy and the Kyoto School: A Summary and Evaluation. *Dao, 13*, 469-489.

Rosenthal, D. M. (1998). Two concepts of consciousness. In *Consciousness and Emotion in Cognitive Science* (pp. 1-31). Routledge.

Russell, B. (1905). On denoting. *Mind, 14*(56), 479-493.

Russell, B. (1911, January). On the relations of universals and particulars. In *Proceedings of the Aristotelian society* (Vol. 12, pp. 1-24). Aristotelian Society, Wiley.

Russell, B. (2009). *Philosophical essays*. Routledge.

Sartre, J. P. (2015). Being and nothingness. *Central works of philosophy: the twentieth century: Moore to popper, 4*, 155.

Sartre, J. P. (2015). *Sketch for a Theory of the Emotions*. Routledge.

Sartre, J. P., Richmond, S., & Moran, R. (2022). *Being and nothingness: An essay in phenomenological ontology*. Routledge.

Scarborough, M. (2000). In the Beginning: Hebrew God and Zen Nothingness. *Buddhist-Christian Studies, 20*, 191-216.

Schlinger, H. D. (2008). Consciousness is nothing but a word. *Skeptic, 13*(4), 58-63.

Scott, S. (2022). Social nothingness: A phenomenological investigation. *European Journal of Social Theory, 25*(2), 197 216.

Scotus, D., & Scotus, J. D. (1997). *Duns Scotus on the will and morality*. CUA Press.

Sebastian, C. D. (2016). *The cloud of nothingness: The negative way in Nagarjuna and John of the cross* (Vol. 19). Springer.

Shakespeare, W. (1995). *Much ado about nothing* (C. T. Watts, Ed.). Wordsworth Classic.

Shaviro, S. (2012). *Without criteria: Kant, whitehead, deleuze, and aesthetics.* MIT press.

Sheridan, A. (2003). *Michel Foucault: The will to truth.* Routledge.

Shien, G. M. (1951). Being and Nothingness in Greek and Ancient Chinese Philosophy. *Philosophy East and West, 1*(2), 16-24.

Şimşek, O. (2019). Emptiness and Nothingness in OMA's Libraries.

Smith, D. G. (2019). Vulnerability, Dependence, and the Knowledge of God: Reflections on Meister Eckhart and Intellectual Disability. *Medieval Mystical Theology, 28*(2), 97-115.

Smith, D. W. (2014). Gilles deleuze. In *Poststructuralism and Critical Theory's Second Generation* (pp. 91-110). Routledge.

Smith, G. H. (2010). *Atheism: The case against god.* Prometheus Books.

Söderquist, K. B. (2015). Kierkegaard and Existentialism: From Anxiety to Autonomy. *A companion to Kierkegaard*, 81-95.

Solomon, R. C. (1993). The philosophy of emotions. *M. Lewic & Haviland, The Handbook of emotions*, 3.

Sorensen, R. (2003). Nothingness.

Spaeth, J. W. (1942, January). Persius on Epicurus: A note on Satires 3.83-84. In *Transactions and Proceedings of the American Philological Association* (Vol. 73, pp. 119-122). Johns Hopkins University Press, American Philological Association.

Stambaugh, J. (1999). *The formless self.* SUNY Press.

Steffney, J. (1985). Nothingness and death in Heidegger and Zen Buddhism. *The Eastern Buddhist, 18*(1), 90-104.

Stenger, V. J. (2009). *The new atheism: Taking a stand for science and reason.* Prometheus Books.

Suzuki, D. T. (1991). *An introduction to zen buddhism.* Grove Press.

Suzuki, D. T. (2018). *Mysticism: Christian and buddhist.* Routledge.

Suzuki, D. T. (2019). *Zen and Japanese culture* (Vol. 334). Princeton University Press.

Suzuki, S. (1999). *Branching streams flow in the darkness: Zen talks on the sandokai.* University of California Press.

Suzuki, S. (2020). *Zen mind, beginner's mind.* Shambhala Publications.

Tchividjian, T. (2011). Jesus+ Nothing= Everything. *Wheaton, IL: Crossway.*

Trigg, D. (2006). *The aesthetics of decay: Nothingness, nostalgia, and the absence of reason* (Vol. 37). Peter Lang.

Vos, A. (2006). *Philosophy of John Duns Scotus.* Edinburgh University Press.

Wallace, L. (2020). *Karl Barth's concept of nothingness: a critical evaluation.* Peter Lang.

Wargo, R. J. (2005). *The logic of nothingness: A study of Nishida Kitaro.* University of Hawaii Press.

Watson, R. A. (1984). Descartes Knows Nothing. *History of Philosophy Quarterly*, *1*(4), 399-411.

Wider, K. V. (1997). *The bodily nature of consciousness: Sartre and contemporary philosophy of mind.* Cornell University Press.

Wilber, K. (2001). *No boundary: Eastern and Western approaches to personal growth.* Shambhala Publications.

Wilber, K. (2005). Introduction to integral theory and practice. *AQAL: Journal of Integral Theory and Practice*, *1*(1), 2-38.

Williams, B. (1973). Wittgenstein and idealism. *Royal Institute of Philosophy Supplements*, *7*, 76-95.

Wordsworth, W. (1884). *Ode: Intimations of immortality from recollections of early childhood.* D. Lothrop and Company.

Wordsworth, W., & Blunden, E. (1996). *Intimations of immortality.* Phoenix.

Wyschogrod, M. (1989). David K. Coe., Angst and the Abyss: The Hermeneutics of Nothingness. *International Studies in Philosophy*, *21*(1), 73-74.

Zarader, M. (2003). Phenomenality and transcendence. *Transcendence in philosophy and religion*, 106-119.

Printed by Libri Plureos GmbH in Hamburg,
Germany